"PETER GLEN'S BOOK IS A MUST. HIS WRY HUMOR EN-
HANCES EVERY PAGE. READ IT NOW!"
> — Michael Friedheim, Executive Vice-President,
> Melville Corporation

"PERHAPS THE QUALITY REVOLUTION IN CUSTOMER
SERVICE WILL BEGIN WITH PETER GLEN'S ANECDO-
TAL ACCOUNTS OF EXCELLENT AND ATROCIOUS CUS-
TOMER SERVICE."
> — Mark E. Pasquerilla, President,
> Crown America Corporation

"IN A HUMOROUS BUT VERY SPECIFIC WAY, *IT'S NOT
MY DEPARTMENT!* IS A GAME PLAN TO WIN."
> — Ed Carroll, Senior Vice-President,
> Bergner's and Company

"PETER GLEN SHOWS HOW TO CUT THROUGH THE
SMOKESCREEN OF SHODDY CUSTOMER SERVICE. HIS
BOOK IS A TRUE DELIGHT AND RIGHT ON TARGET."
> — Harry Hoffman, former President and CEO,
> Waldenbooks

IT'S NOT MY DEPARTMENT!

HOW AMERICA CAN RETURN TO EXCELLENCE— GIVING AND RECEIVING QUALITY SERVICE

PETER GLEN

BERKLEY BOOKS, NEW YORK

For Sam Dunn—

the best fighter of all

CONTENTS

CONTENTS

Find out what you want,

And how you want it,

And live your whole life

Just that way!

IT'S NOT MY DEPARTMENT!

I. A NATION OF WHINERS

This is the way the world ends
Not with a bang but a whimper.

—T. S. Eliot

THIS JOB SUCKS!

Early one morning in America, hungry, alone, and lost in the land of no customer service, I stumbled into a Dunkin' Donuts in Connecticut. The parking lot was dirty and the trash cans overflowed, but the parking lot was already full of cars and the trash cans would see more, much more, before the day was over. Inside were lines of people smoking cigarettes and wearing parkas, waiting to buy donuts. I waited with them, observing the uncleared counter where I soon would sit to eat my donut. It hadn't been cleared recently, and it wasn't going to be cleared now.

I reached the head of the line, came face to face with a seventeen-year-old girl who had been condemned to serve me. Something in her seventeen-year-old face told me that all was not well in America's service economy. I asked her how she liked her job.

She looked me straight in the eye and said, "It sucks!"

That's service in America. And that's too bad, because we are a "service economy." But we don't give good service, and we don't get it. We expect poor quality and bad service, and we are rarely disappointed.

Instead of fighting, we whine. Those who provide service whine about the people they hire and the people they hire pass the whining right on to their customers. Those who buy service—customers—whine right back.

We are a nation of whiners.

We are basically a nation of individuals, but we whine as a group. We try to top each other's horror stories of service at every dinner party. In whining, we are united. Our national anthem is "It's Not My Department!"

It is the shout of the millions who serve customers.

A waitress screams in a food court in a mall, where a woman is about to share a salad with her aged father, "Stop him! No sharing! Restaurant policy! If he takes one bite of that salad, I'll have to charge you for it!"

Customers whine too.

More than 450 million people flew on airlines in 1988; only 21,000 complained. In one month 200,000 passengers had their baggage mishandled—lost, delayed, pilfered, or damaged. Only 156 passengers bothered to register complaints. We aren't even a nation of complainers!

Today you might want ice cream. But the girl who works in the Swensen's ice cream store in the mall has her finger almost all the way up her nose. (S'not her department.)

You are about to buy a wedding ring. But the jewelry saleswoman at Fortunoff's is filing her nails over the diamond case.

The man in the Chinese laundry will neatly launder and fold your shirts and then smash every button.

A Wall Street salesman slams the phone down in your ear the instant he perceives you do not want what he is selling.

A voice answers the phone when you call a bike shop to see if they are open. "What a stupid question!" says the voice. "Would I be answering the phone if we were closed?"

Today your accountant will file your tax forms late. The furniture man will not show up for the third time, and for the third time you will have stayed home from work for nothing.

The contractor working on your house tries to conceal a pipe sticking out of your wall by putting a plant in front of it. You overhear him say, about you, "They probably won't notice it."

If you provide a service today, you'll have to put up with customers, patients, or students. But if you serve the public and you hate your job, what do you do about it? You whine. You are an employee in Hell, but you do nothing about it. Occasionally you might complain, but you won't demand and you certainly won't fight.

We are a nation of wimps. As providers we expect to give poor service. As customers we expect to receive it. It is terrible to give and to receive bad service. We tolerate it. Then we pay for it. And then we whine.

I was antagonizing a desk clerk at a mammoth new Marriott in Orlando by simply trying to check in. This girl was coming apart before my very eyes because she couldn't find my name anywhere in the reservations computer. She jabbed at the machine's buttons, stared into its screen, asked a colleague, and even challenged a supervisor. Nobody could find my reservation. I finally said, "You don't seem to be having a very good day."

She looked up and said, "I was until *you* showed up!"

You've met this person a thousand times. She doesn't give a damn and the fact that she doesn't give a damn is the main reason there is no service in the service economy.

The time is right for revolution. We've hit bottom. Our leaders don't lead. Our products don't work. We make cars that fall apart and sweaters whose sleeves unravel before we get them home from the store. U.S. manufacturers spend an estimated twenty cents of every dollar just fixing defective products. Providers of service spend an estimated thirty cents of every dollar correcting errors and answering complaints about service that wasn't right in the first place. We live in a "service economy" but there is no service. Nobody gives a damn. "It's not my department." Nothing is anybody's department any more. Servers don't serve. And customers put up with it. They don't expect service, and they don't get service.

If you confront the owner of a fleet of filthy taxis anywhere in America, he'll tell you, "It's not worth washing them from October to May because they just get dirty again, and besides, look at the kind of trash I got working for me. Put one of these guys in a clean taxi and by the time he stops at Wendy's three times, it will be filled halfway up to his knees with hamburger wrappers and the crossword puzzle and Coke cans."

When service providers do not bother to take baths, or wash their hair, or get dressed decently, or clean their cabs, they usually hate themselves and their work. And that is *their* problem.

No wonder taxis, schools, and all the roads in America are disfigured. People who don't think much of themselves usually don't mind uglifying the look of the nation or the Earth.

But when a taxi driver drives around town in a taxi filled with trash because he hates himself, and you have to sit there with him, that's bad service, and that is *your* problem.

You could have looked and sniffed inside before you got in. Or you can start berating him about his taxi. Or you can just stay sitting there, holding your nose and thinking, *This isn't so bad. This is America and this is service and this is the way it is.*

The sign on Harry S. Truman's desk said, THE BUCK

STOPS HERE. He was taking responsibility for service to his "customers."

Good service does exist in America. Some companies provide it even without making their customers fight for it. The names are familiar and admired: Nordstrom, Federal Express, Disney, Stew Leonard's, L. L. Bean, Lands' End. There are quite a few in other countries. We recognize good service, and when it happens we practically worship it, but the list is short.

Today you might get a delivery from Lands' End. Every item will be tagged, "Guaranteed. Period." If you buy a skirt at The Limited, the tag will tell you, "No sale is ever final."

Nordstrom will take back anything for any reason at any time, and every salesperson working there has the *authority*—and the order—to do it. Immediately. Then they will send you a Christmas card.

You will hear CEO's bang on podiums in major meetings trying to convince everyone in the audience how much they believe in customer service. It's a priority, it's a mission statement, it's a target, it's a goal. Then he'll go back to the office and cut expenses by firing staff.

"Service" is the hottest subject in business right now, but most of the service is lip service, not "customer service."

THE SIGN OF THE CUSTOMER

You can get good service if you fight for it. A revolution can start with a single individual. When second-grade teacher Carole Gilmore drove her 1930 Model "A" Ford into a Phoenix gas station one bright May day, a revolution began. The pump station was "self-service" so she filled her tank with gas, but as she was replacing the nozzle she suddenly noticed the price on the pump. It was two cents higher than the posted price on the huge sign on the street. Carole, the customer, pointed out this discrepancy and asked how much she owed based on the price advertised on the sign.

"Sorry, lady," the station attendant said, and shrugged his shoulders (shoulder shrugging is a certain clue that the curtain is about to go up on "It's not my department"). "The price just went up a few hours ago and I haven't had a chance to get up there and change the sign yet."

This is where the world ends for most customers; beaten, discouraged, and depressed, they dig down deep and come up with the difference. But not Carole. In her best class-if-I-could-have-your-attention voice, loud enough so other customers lining up behind her could hear her perfectly, she announced, "Young man, look at me." And then she did a revolutionary thing.

She held up her right hand and made a letter C with her thumb and forefinger. Then she moved the "C" sign up to her eye and looked through it straight at the attendant.

"I am the customer," she continued, "and this C stands for *customer*. I refuse to be victimized by you or your sign or your system around here. You certainly had a chance to change the prices on the pumps, but if you'd thought about it, you'd have changed the road sign first, in honor of your customers.

"You have two choices. I am willing to pay you either your advertised price right now, or else you have exactly three minutes to get that gasoline back out of my tank before I drive out of here without paying you anything. Which is it going to be?"

The chastened attendant cowered before the "C" sign and accepted the advertised price. He thought she was a bitch. Carole knew she was a *customer*.

It was a mystical experience.

The "C" sign is the sign of the customer, and it can also be the sign of the revolution. Wouldn't it be great if we were a nation of fighters, if 250 million Americans started rioting for good service, for caring enough to carry out a breathtaking revolution?

This book will tell you how to become a better customer and a better provider of service. But no book can make you stop whining. Only you can act. No "motivator," preacher, play, TV show, guru, father, mother, teacher, or child can make you act. So you can read this book or throw it out, enjoy it, or ignore it or agree with it, or you can take it to heart and open up to many new possibilities. This should be an adventure for you. So bring your best self and some courage—this is not a rehearsal. Life is in session now!

Dr. Mattingly—you'll meet her a few pages from now—always taught me that you must do the best you can, whether it moves the majority of people or not, even if you only reach three out of a hundred.

So this book is dedicated to the three out of a hundred who care enough to fight, who *live* every day of their lives, no matter what it is that they do.

Fighters never say, "It's not my department!"

Life is their department.

So why don't you just stop whining, and join the revolution?

II. MOTIVATION NEVER ENDS

Some people are self-motivated. You may meet four or five in your life—if you're lucky. Here's one of them:

For years I had heard about a cheap restaurant called the Original Pantry in downtown Los Angeles. This place had remained continuously open, twenty-four hours a day since 1924—even though they changed locations once, during the forties. During the move they had kept the griddle hot in both locations while they removed a stack of half-cooked pancakes from the old place, carried them across the street, and finished cooking them in the new location. That's continuity.

I went and sat down at the counter, waiting for the experience to begin. It did. I sensed, then felt, then saw a major personality moving down the counter towards me. I could feel self-confidence coming my way.

I often ask whoever is serving me what is best to eat, which room to stay in, where I should sit in the theater, and so on. It's usually a waste of time. Ask most food service types what they recommend, and they will giggle and say, "Everything is good"—always a lie—or "They don't feed us what you eat."

But this eminence behind the counter seemed different to me. And she was. I asked her, "What is the best thing in the place?" and she promptly said, "I am!"

This woman respected herself. She didn't hate what she was doing and she didn't resent me. She was motivated.

But most people need help. Helen Keller said, "Science may have found a cure for most evils; but it has found no remedy for the worst of them all—the apathy of human beings."

GETTING MOTIVATED

Most people don't get motivated until they get into a crisis. Some stop smoking when their doctor tells them they've got three months to live. Madeline Pflaumbaum started Mothers Against Drunk Driving after her son was killed by a drunk driver. Rick Hansen pushed his wheelchair forty thousand miles around the world after he was paralyzed from the waist down in an accident. People stop having unsafe sex or using dirty needles when someone they know dies of AIDS. Greg Louganis dove to win gold medals right after he cracked his skull on the diving board.

Nike's people got motivated after success made them smug and they started repeating themselves. Reebok suddenly pounded them out of the lead. Nike woke up and started fighting, invented the slogan "JUST DO IT," and recaptured first place.

Motivated people have motives. A motive is "something (as a need or desire) that causes a person to act." If action is the aim of life, then it's being motivated that will get you there. Unmotivated folks do not move. There are a lot of them, and they are a sorry spectacle, because they do not seem to care enough to translate their lives into action. Motivated people move, they get things done, and they live each day of their life as if it mattered. You cannot *be* motivated by someone else; it is not something that happens *to* you. You can be informed and inspired by others, but *you* must motivate *yourself*.

On the Isle of Capri you can still go swimming at certain times. The water is fairly clean until the outgoing tide from Naples brings a sea of garbage floating out to Capri and drives all sensible bathers out of the water.

One day we found ourselves a crystal-clear cove with just one other boat, a large yacht full of chic Italian sunworshippers, probably from Naples. They were preparing lunch on deck, and we watched while they opened and emptied cans of tuna for their Salade Niçoise. Then the woman who was preparing lunch for guests picked up three glistening tin tuna cans and threw them into the Tyrrhenian Sea.

I was motivated. Without even thinking, I dove into the water and managed to grab all three cans on their way down to the bottom of the cove, where they would undoubtedly have remained long enough for Rome to rise and fall a dozen times. I climbed up the ladder of their boat onto their main deck, where they all sat astonished while I put the three tin tuna cans back on their dining table.

Just then I realized what I was doing and that if I had had my wits about me, I probably wouldn't have done it.

But I had done it, and the point was made, and I dove back into the water and swam back to our boat. Not a word was exchanged all afternoon as, side by side, we two boats shared the pristine beauty of our little cove. One never knows if throwing little fits like that is actually helpful or just dangerous, but when one does them one knows the purity of individual motivation in action.

I don't believe mob motivation works. People do indulge themselves in schools and groups and videotapes and handbooks; they enroll in expensive courses; they enjoy feeling sorry for themselves and sharing sorrows; they chant mantras and automatic congregational responses. All of this may be innocuous entertainment, and it is big business, but afterwards these graduates emerge filled with temporary energy and an intrusive desire to enroll everyone else in the same experience. They go around raving for a few minutes or a few days, and then the fire dies.

Many professional "motivators" are con men and generalists. They "motivate everyone" at once, and there is no such thing as "everyone." What works for one person won't work for another. Motivation is an *individual* matter every time.

In my job, I urge my clients to ignore their own opinion of themselves. I try to see more in them than they do, and get them to concentrate on doing better. I get them to remember any who ever "motivated" them. Surely almost everyone has had a teacher or a coach or a mother who said to them, "I don't agree with you. That's not the best you can do. You can do more, much more, do it again, do it better, stop whining. More!" If you can recall this experience, and can recreate it now, you will be starting to motivate yourself.

I first learned this soaring sense of life and all its possibilities from my beloved college professor, Alethea Mattingly.

She didn't tolerate my own opinion of myself. She didn't like other people's opinions of me either. And she told me so. She changed my life. She got it started. She's out in Arizona now, celebrating an unknown birthday, and although she is almost legally blind, she is learning German. When I recently asked her why she was learning German, she said, "Because I don't know it."

I was a mediocre complainer who had just enrolled in the University of Arizona. I had a fairly low opinion of myself, and therefore a very low opinion of what life was going to be like. But I had paid my enrollment fees, and therefore I was a customer. It was then that I came face to face with Dr. Mattingly.

When I first met Alethea Mattingly, she was teaching a course called "Oral Interpretation of Literature." I had had a dim idea that I wanted to be a performer, so I had signed up. Dr. Mattingly was really teaching "life," but we spent the time learning how to perform literature by reading it aloud.

I had never learned to take charge and focus in on what I was doing. Like most people, I just dealt with whatever came my way, and life was happening *to* me rather than the other way around. I had possibilities and Dr. Mattingly knew it, but I couldn't yet concentrate my way to an A in anything.

Dr. Mattingly had a dreadful reputation. It was thought that she was tough on all her students, and the rumor was that she gave out only A's or F's. It seemed she didn't believe in mediocre grades.

I studied with her for three years before the day she called me out of the classroom, alone, into her office. She said, "Sit down. I have something to tell you which you won't like hearing. In fact, you probably won't like me for a few months after I tell you. But you need to know this.

"You are a talented but intolerant person. You think more about yourself than you do about other people. You don't have enough reverence for life. You must learn that *everything* is interesting, even each amoeba in the ocean, because God made every one. And yet you want to be a performer. I can teach you to perform, but you will never be a great performer if you do not reach the audience. You need to start learning *love* and *respect* for other people, and when you do, only then will you communicate."

She was right. She was telling me what she believed, but she was telling me in terms of myself.

Many years later, I went back to school and asked her why she was always so demanding, even on students who didn't want anything from her classes except to survive and get out, while she *always* did her best. I asked her why.

"I always try to see more in other people than they see in themselves," she said. And when she said that I knew how she had motivated me.

Now I try to do that with others. I try to see more in the person giving me customer service because otherwise I'm not going to get much except abuse.

I try to inspire classes or mobs of executives or service providers by not accepting their opinions of themselves, which are usually lower than they ought or need to be —which explains why most customers and service providers are mediocre.

I want them to concentrate on what they're doing, and to love themselves.

We need people to admire, but it's hard today. Runners are full of steroids, baseball players gamble on their own teams, hotel queens cheat, religious leaders steal, and more than a few mayors deal drugs. Oil companies spill, infecting the planet. Dictators buy thousands of pairs of shoes. They all get away with it because we only whine, and there are very few role models to look up to.

While waiters are waiting on me, I wish they would act like that was what they wanted to be doing, at least during my meal. If they were doing something they wanted to do, they would be living in the present and enjoying it and doing a better job, instead of wishing they were doing something else and treating me as if I were the one preventing them from doing it.

Some people are filled with abstract longings, but they never actually live the way they want to. If you're not doing something you really want to do, you can't be motivated.

I once knew a man who was chairman of Dayton's in Minneapolis. He was enormously successful, ultimately responsible for the motivation of twenty thousand people, and he was good at it. I also thought he would be happy motivating millions, but I was wrong. One night we were having a drink at a bar in Minneapolis, talking about the business, and suddenly this man lapsed into silence. I looked at him and he looked worried.

"What's wrong?" I asked.

He turned to me and said, with real sincerity, "I think I could have been a great tenor."

He was good at what he did and he was famous and had lots of money. He certainly knew if he could have been a tenor or not. But whenever it was that he realized what he really wanted to be, it was too late.

The first big executive I ever met was the general merchandise manager of a huge department store, L. S. Ayres, in Indianapolis. I expected a hero, but what I got instead was a free tuna sandwich with a chronic whiner. He whined about the lunch, and the weather, and his job, and I'd been thinking this man was going to be inspiring, powerful, and enthusiastic! He complained about his wife, his routine, and even his store. I listened to this because I was shocked and surprised, and because I was hungry and poor.

When his tirade ended, I asked him, "If you dislike all this so much, why don't you get out?"

I will always remember what he said.

"I've only got fifteen years to go."

Don't you know a lot of people like that? They are not motivated and they surely cannot motivate anyone else. They will all be lousy customers and lousy service providers.

When I was in my twenties I spent every summer living in Italy. I rode a bicycle, played the piano, wrote stories, and generally indulged myself. At the end of the summer I would come back and work hard for the next nine months. One year, after I had just returned, I met a merchant who asked me about this.

"Is it true you go to Italy every summer?"

"Yes," I said.

"I just envy you so much," he said. "How do you do it?"

Being young and sarcastic, I said, "I get in a cab and just go to the airport and get on a plane."

He lost his temper: "Don't be such a smartass." Then he got started on all the things he was burdened with. He couldn't go to Italy because he had a mortgage, kitchen appliances, cars, expensive watches, a wife, a mother-in-law, and three daughters in college.

When he got done with all this, I said, "Your daughters aren't in college now. It's still summer vacation. Where are they?"

"They're in Italy," he said rather sheepishly.

For a time I also lived in Australia. Following my first presentation over there, which had thrilled me—and, I thought, the audience—there was a cocktail hour. A local buyer, who was drunk, came up to me and said, "You're so enthusiastic! But that's because you've only been here a week. Come back next year and we'll see how enthusiastic you are!"

During the following year I went to Melbourne, Launceston, Brisbane, Perth, Fiji, Surfer's Paradise, and Coober Pedy, the latter being a town in the "dead heart" of Australia where it is so hot that the opal miners live in caves that have been dynamited out of the ground.

And after that first wonderful year, I was back on stage in Sydney using every one of my adventures. Yes, that same buyer was there too. I was still enthusiastic and she was still drunk.

Get those scared, stuck, paralyzing people out of your life. Demotivated people hold you back. They want you, if at all, on their level. Getting rid of them is very motivating.

DEALING WITH "NO!"

I hate the word *no*. It is the most demotivating word in English. You will hear it throughout your life as a customer and as a service provider, and the only thing that matters is how you act when you hear it. It is an easy, cheap, unproductive word. It is the favorite word of failures. It is a short, sharp, frequent form of "It's not my department."

When you hear the word *no*, it is time to start making the C sign. That is the only way that the word *no* can be motivating.

A buyer might have a bright idea: "Let's have a 'Santa Fe' shop."

"No."

Or: "Let's match every dime a customer gives us and give it all to the homeless for Christmas."

"No."

When David Sarnoff of R.C.A. was first told about television, he announced that it was a scientific and economic impossibility.

"No."

When Lee Iacocca said to Chrysler, "We're going to have convertibles," the technical people said "No," and the finance people said "No," and the dealers said "No," and the salesmen said "No." But the customers said "Yes!" and, fortunately, Lee Iacocca said, "We're having them!" He told his people to get a can opener if they had to and take the top off the car and stop giving him the runaround, because they were going to build convertibles.

John Jay is the creative director for Bloomingdale's, and he had a hunch in the back of his mind a few years ago that an obscure foreign movie entitled *Chariots of Fire* portrayed a stupendous menswear look that was right for the times. He went to the merchandise managers and suggested that they put together a storewide promotion around the film. The managers said they had never heard of the movie, this was not England, and this is not the 1930's. The buyers wouldn't go for it.

John Jay decided he didn't like the answer "No" and that they were wrong and he was right. But he was not the boss. So he had to persuade them. He went to the movie theater across the street, paid for a private screening of the film at ten o'clock in the morning and got all the buyers to come see it. They loved it. The store put together one of its most successful promotions, which happened to debut two days before *Chariots of Fire* won the Academy Award for "Best Foreign Film" of that year. No one knew for certain that it would win, or that the soundtrack would become as popular as it did or that the fashion look would become so successful. Bloomingdale's had it first because John Jay found a way of changing "No" to "Yes."

Mark Twain said, "The man with a new idea is a crank until the idea succeeds."

Most new ideas, even great ones, are greeted with "No." When Beethoven wrote the *Eroica* Symphony and

broke every rule, the orchestra said, "We can't play it."
When Stravinsky premiered *The Rite of Spring*, the critics
declared him insane. When Marcel DuChamp painted
Nude Descending a Staircase, No. 2, everybody decided
it was the worst picture ever painted before someone
recognized it as a turning point in art history. When
Freud described the unconscious, the conscious world
said "No." When James Joyce changed literature forever
by writing in the stream-of-consciousness technique,
everybody declared "No." And in the last chapter of his
book *Ulysses*, the leading character says the word *yes*
several dozen times.

Yes is more motivating than *No*.

SEARCHING FOR "YES!"

I just love the word *yes*! When I see a door that says NO
or DON'T or STOP I want to push on it immediately. One
time I got "backstage" at Disneyland this way, in spite
of an awesome security system that keeps "guests" out
of "backstage." There are doors hidden everywhere so
that customers will never see a "character" in costume
in the wrong area. "Onstage" it is against the rules to be
a Disney character in half a costume, smoking a cigarette.

Disneyland's customers are buying happiness and paying for perfection and they usually get it.

One day I pushed on a Disney door and suddenly found myself in a nonfantasy room full of word processing equipment and fifteen executive secretaries who were dressed like executive secretaries. On the first desk was a crystal vase with a real red rose in it. The woman sitting behind the desk was somewhat amazed to see me, but she didn't let Disney down when I asked her, "Who gave you the rose?" She said, "Mickey Mouse!"

I asked her, "Why?" And she said, "Because Mickey Mouse loves me. Now I need to ask how you managed to get in here."

This was great customer service. Most people would have called security and had me thrown back out into the fantasy world. Instead she preserved the Disney image. And did her job.

When I was a sophomore in high school, I got a load of samples from my father's sportswear company and drove up to G. Fox, an independently owned department store in Hartford, Connecticut. At that time the store was run by an octogenarian named Beatrice Auerbach. She was quite well known in the trade, and I always wanted to meet famous people. The buyer for the store said she didn't want my line and basically told me good-bye.

"I'm sorry you don't want to buy my line," I said. "Where is Mrs. Auerbach's office?"

The buyer looked at me like I was crazy. She couldn't believe I had the cheek to ask such a question, but she pointed up and said, simply, "Upstairs."

I sprinted up the stairs and found myself in a large, serious-looking hallway paneled in rich, dark wood for which it seemed half the trees in Connecticut had been slaughtered. A starchy secretary kept guard from behind a huge wooden desk in front of an enormous set of carved-wood doors. As I headed straight for them the secretary said, "Where are you going?"

"I would like to see Mrs. Auerbach," I said.

She panicked. "No. You can't go in there. You don't have an appointment."

By that time I was already inside the room, and there at the end of this very long table sat a very small, very old lady doing, as I had suspected, nothing.

"Can I talk to you?" I asked.

"Yes," she said. "Who are you?"

I told her I was representing the Glen of Michigan line, but that I had really just wanted to come up and meet her.

"I'm so glad they sent you in," she said. "Nobody comes to see me because they think they can't get in."

STAYING MOTIVATED

There is a little-known ritual that takes place in big department stores. This ritual is devised to motivate employees and to create sales. It is called the "walkthrough." It is a ceremonial occasion of considerable fear and trembling amongst the ranks when "top" or "upper" management comes through to conduct an inspection.

This inspection is important. Business depends on what they see and do. It usually takes place just before the public arrives for a major merchandising promotion such as "Back to School," or a new branch opening in a suburb.

Christmas is the retail event in which the hopes and fears of all the years are met in one mighty month— December. The last eight weeks of the year bring in a third of annual revenues and half, or more, of net income. So there are many major "walk-throughs" before Christmas, and the platoons of executives impress the multitudes as they make their way across their kingdoms.

> 'Twas the night before Christmas and all through the store,
> The "walk-through" approached and inspected each floor.
> The buyers were nervously lining the aisles,
> With assistants behind them and uncertain smiles.
> The tension was high amongst all of the throng,
> As the moguls walked by to see what might be wrong.

At one large department store, the major majesty nodded and smiled and observed and progressed down the aisles, but he did not speak. He persevered until the end, then turned, then paused. It was time to witness a great piece of possible motivation; a precise mix of judgment, praise, and criticism, inspiring in expression— enough to make mountains of merchandise move.

He spoke. All listened.

"This is wonderful," he said. "It is neat and orderly, correct, complete. We are thoroughly planned and presented. There are no problems. I'd say after looking at this that we were going to have a very nice Christmas.

"So, I am going to ask you to do it again. Do it over. Mess it up. Give it a good swift kick. Add an idea or two. Make me laugh. Do something silly. Take a risk.

Get my attention. Don't lose a thing you have accomplished, but don't stop here.

"Nice is not enough. We need to make our Christmas great.

"So, do it again.

"And thank you. Merry Christmas."

And then the procession moved on into the mystical distance, leaving Christmas behind in the hands and hearts of the people they had just been paid to motivate.

The excellent people he had just addressed were challenged, excited, and motivated. They had received a balanced measure of criticism and recognition. They had been shown the careful blend of discipline and creativity. They had been motivated.

The mediocre people were mad. They broke into feverish whining, having heard only the hard part of the criticism—that they had to do it over—and not knowing what to do about it.

The majority stood aside, as majorities do, just waiting for Christmas to hit them.

Motivation is not a steady flame. It flickers and dies down, and sometimes flares again; the fire needs fuel.

Often.

I learned this lesson about persistence from three old cronies who worked together behind the hat counter at Bullock's in California. One day I said to them, "You ladies are selling hats. You should be *wearing* hats. You would get so much attention, and people would be entertained." Then I told them that I would be *coming back* at noon and, "You'd better have those hats on."

That turned out to be the most important thing I said, because all that mattered to them was that they were going to be checked on! They said, "Who are you?" I was feeling mischievous and said, "You'll find out."

Well, I returned at noon and they were resplendent

in their hats! "We've had some really great sales," they said, "and people come up and say, 'You look just terrific and wonderful!' "

I told them, "I'm coming back at five-thirty." They said, "All right. Shall we keep our hats on?" "Oh yes!" I said.

I came back at five-thirty, and sure enough, hat department sales were way up. In fact, they'd had one of their best days ever! These women were laughing and carrying on and having the most fun they'd ever had on their jobs.

But then—I went back the next morning. No hats!

"Where are your hats?" I asked. To which they replied, "We didn't know you were coming back."

It is harder to maintain good service than it is to achieve it. In fact, some of the "gods" are being attacked right now.

On October 31, 1517, Martin Luther attacked the unattackable Catholic Church of Rome by posting his revolutionary 95 Theses on the door of the Palast Church in Wittenberg. This small customer protest started the Reformation and diluted the success of the Catholic Church.

Four hundred and forty-five years later, on February 20, 1990, *The Wall Street Journal* ran a front-page article attacking the unattackable citadel of customer service in America, Nordstrom stores. The headline read "At Nordstrom Stores, Service Comes First—But at a Big Price." The article revealed trouble in paradise, including unhappiness amongst the "Nordies" and a possible work action against the store which could cost the management at least $15 million in back wages.

Suddenly *Business Week* runs a story headlined "Land's End Looks a Bit Frayed at the Edges," citing the biggest earnings slide ever, too many catalogs, tired styles, and too few customers. A crisis of service. The article ends, "the preppies from Dodgeville had better roll up their sleeves. They're in for a street fight."

And even L. L. Bean, for many years a near-religious experience in customer service, has trouble keeping the service pace. In 1988, dissatisfied customers returned $82 million dollars worth of goods. They are hastily retraining 3,200 employees in techniques that improve customer service and quality.

Motivation never ends. No one is motivated permanently. You need to keep pursuing it, possibly forever.

There is a lake in Africa in a crater thirty-five miles long. The lake is called Lake Natron. As your Jeep edges down the crater walls, you realize that the huge pink cloud you see on the lake is a cloud of birds! One hundred thousand flamingos live in the shallows of Lake Natron. As you get out of the Jeep and walk toward the shoreline, at a certain distance every one of the one hundred thousand flamingos will take exactly one step back into the lake. If you stop and wait quietly, they will all take one step back towards you. But you and these flamingos will never actually meet. Motivation, like Lake Natron's flamingos, is always one step ahead of you.

People keep searching for motivation. When Gertrude Stein was dying, Alice B. Toklas rushed to her bedside and exclaimed, "Gertrude, Gertrude, what is the answer?" And Gertrude Stein replied, "What is the question?"

Motivation is like that.

Rainer Maria Rilke said that you can never know the answers, so therefore you must learn to love the questions.

Motivation is like that.

Robin Goldman, a nine-year-old girl who had leukemia, made a greeting card with a man standing on a mountain top, throwing up a rope, preparing to climb onto a passing cloud. The message was: "When you get to the top of the mountain, keep right on climbing!"

Motivation is like that.

Life is like that.

You can be like that too. To be motivated is to be alive.

III. TALES OF DISASTER

"THOSE BASTARDS DO THIS ALL THE TIME"

If you ever go to Las Vegas, you're just asking for service nightmares, unless you think big free smorgasbords are a service. So take a sense of humor with you. "Service" in Vegas includes everything from a waitress in a mini-toga and black eye shadow, pouring wine from a Naugahyde flask into your glass and saying, "Hi, I'm Linda. I'll be your slave tonight," to the genuine adventure of being checked into your room by a bellboy-actor-dancer-model and, yes, possibly, slave.

One such bellboy-actor-dancer-model and I finally reached my room in the Hilton Hotel in Las Vegas at the end of a fourteen-minute walk through a purple-carpeted hall with orange cafeteria-steakhouse wallpaper and all of last night's room-service trays lining the walls. Opening the door, we discovered two people in the bed. The bellboy-actor-dancer-model surveyed the scene and announced, "Those bastards at check-in do this all the time."

So I called up the front desk and said, "The bellman tells me you 'bastards' are always checking customers into occupied rooms." The front desk clerk started whining about computers and a "full house," but eventually he told the bellman to drag me and my luggage to a different room.

This one looked as though it had never been cleaned. There were towels in the bed, a half-empty jar of Vaseline on the sofa, luggage tickets strewn about, and hairs in the bathtub. Las Vegas was obviously everything it was promised to be for somebody.

I called up the desk again and I said, "Those 'bastards' the bellman has been telling me about have checked me into an unoccupied room all right, but it's not clean."

"Why don't you call housekeeping?" the desk clerk suggested.

"Why don't *you* call housekeeping?" I responded.

That launched us into an irrelevant debate about checkout time and how I was early and so forth. There weren't any other rooms to choose from, so I finally persuaded this man to get a maid into the room to muck it out. While I was waiting, I turned on the television. It worked! There was supposed to be a television programming guide in the room, but I couldn't find it. I did find a sign that said, IF ANYTHING IS MISSING, CALL THE ASSISTANT MANAGER. So I dialed up the assistant manager. I told her I needed the guide to television.

"Could you describe it to me?" she asked. "I don't know what you mean."

"How can I describe something that's missing?" I asked. "It's the television guide that's supposed to be in my room and I'm supposed to call you about if it isn't."

"You don't have to get so huffy," she said. "It's only my first week."

When the maid finally showed up, I told her that there wasn't any of their complimentary shampoo in the bathroom.

She heaved a sigh. "Some days we have it and some days we don't. They just never give us enough shampoo." (Who is "*they*"? Usually, it's anyone except the person you're speaking to.)

It took me forty-five minutes to get settled into this establishment, and on the way I alienated most of the people I met, but I finally got what I was paying for. No sooner had I settled down than the phone rang. It was the manager. He wanted to know "if everything was all right?" I hate this habit. I wish managers and waiters would stop interrupting me to ask, "Is everything all right?" If they did their jobs right in the first place, they'd be the first to know, and they wouldn't need to ask.

Imagine this event if I hadn't complained.

I would be, like most customers, sitting in the first room waiting for "Honey and Honey" to finish, clean up, pack, and check out, having already tipped the bellboy-actor-dancer-model. I wouldn't have called housekeeping but might have cleaned the room myself, and lived there TV-guideless, soapless, and hopeless in Las Vegas.

But instead, I did complain.

Getting a better hotel room may not be a matter of life and death, but getting a better heart transplant might be.

THE WORST SERVICE STORY I EVER HEARD

New hires at British Airways are asked to think like customers. Michael Bruce, senior manager of corporate development, once hosted a meeting of about eighty new employees. He asked them to tell their best experience as a customer and their worst.

"I got many long descriptions of their worst experience," he recalled. "Then, when I asked, 'What about the best one?' everyone said, 'I've never had one.' I said, 'Surely there must be somebody here who's had a really great service experience.' Out of eighty people, only three hands finally crept up."

When customers have an adequate experience, they're satisfied, and they usually forget it. But people remember bad service forever. They form their opinion of entire companies or careers based on their worst customer experience. They remember every name and detail and they love to tell how they suffered.

But every now and then a story surfaces which is so horrible that people don't even repeat it. This is the worst story about customer service I have ever heard. It's about Fred Hankin, a 66-year-old Army veteran from San Jose,

California, who was nostalgic for his home town of New York and decided to pay a visit—possibly his last. He'd been sick for a long time with diabetes and cancer. His daughter, Sheila Byers, and son-in-law were going to accompany him. Fred's legs had been amputated some years earlier along with his hips and tailbone, and he felt he needed extra assistance.

They booked round-trip coach seats on Pan Am from San Francisco to New York. Sheila says she told Pan Am when she made the reservations that her father has to sit on a customized prosthetic pillow to keep from toppling over. Sheila made arrangements with the airline for her father to be pre-boarded and for her to be assigned a seat adjacent to him in the bulkhead row where it would be easier to maneuver him in and out of the seat. She had to be there to help him eat and use his portable urinal in privacy without bothering any of the other passengers. She also ordered a diabetic meal for him, and Pan Am promised priority unloading for their luggage, including Fred's wheelchair, when they arrived.

When they got to San Francisco Airport, Sheila says the gate attendants put Fred on a dollylike aisle chair, a cross between a baggage cart and a wheelchair, with no supports or straps to keep him in place, and wheeled him "like a sack of potatoes" onto the plane. The cabin attendant was so clumsy lifting him into the seat that Fred's pants fell off, exposing him to the other passengers. By then Pan Am had lost Fred's prosthetic pillow so he couldn't sit up during the flight.

When the plane arrived in New York, the baggage people couldn't find the wheelchair. For almost three hours, a porter helped push Fred around the airport in a courtesy wheelchair and watched to keep him from falling over while Sheila and her husband tried to get Pan Am employees to locate his own wheelchair. In some back room baggage office, Sheila says a disinterested clerk finally gave up, telling her, "All we can do is fax San Francisco to see if it's still there. There's nothing else we can do. Now you'll have to leave. We're closed. And please shut the door behind you!"

Finally the porter had a brainstorm. He remembered an elevator which was used to move large pieces of baggage. He checked it, and sure enough, that was where the wheelchair had been abandoned.

Sheila says the airline never did find the prosthetic pillow. Fred had to spend the next four days of his nostalgic trip home on his back in a hotel room or lying down in the back seat of a car. He developed bleeding bedsores.

The climax of this nightmare began on the trip back to California. The flight was delayed taking off. Sheila says she asked the gate attendants if there was some place where her father could lie down while they waited. "They offered to let him use a sofa in the first-class lounge, but my father didn't want to be laid out in public like that and they said they had no alternative."

After Fred waited in agony for three hours, Pan Am announced that the plane would be delayed another three and one-half hours. They finally rebooked Fred, Sheila, and her husband onto another flight.

When Sheila asked the ticket agent about all the special arrangements she'd made for Fred, he handed her a computer printout and told her, "Just show this to the gate agents and they'll take care of everything."

When it came time to board, Sheila says the attendants pushed Fred onto the plane ahead of the other passengers in another one of those baggage-cart chairs. But the plane was booked solid and the cabin crew wouldn't honor the previous assignment to bulkhead seats. So they left Fred teetering on this cart in the aisle and on display for forty-five minutes while the rest of the passengers were boarding. The gate agent argued with her, saying,

"You'll have to take whatever seats are empty or get off the plane. If he's that sick, he should be in the hospital."

A sympathetic passenger finally offered to surrender his bulkhead seat, but Sheila got more abuse when she explained to the attendants that she also needed the seat next to her father so she could help him eat and go to the bathroom. She says she overheard an exasperated agent tell the cabin crew members nearby, "If she opens her mouth again I want her kicked off the plane."

Fred Hankin and his daughter filed a lawsuit against the airline. Says Sheila, "They treated us like we were getting on the train to Auschwitz. It shouldn't have happened and I want to know how Pan Am allowed it to."

BAD ADS AND OTHER BAD BEGINNINGS

A lot of disasters start before the customer ever appears. Advertising, for instance, is often bad service. It means well, but so many of its promises turn out to be so false that the advertiser would have been better off (and more honest) to cancel the ads, pocket the money, and let the

customer suffer bad service without the added indignity
of having been lied to.

Imagine reading this garbage in the *New York
Times*—an "ad" for the Trump Tower shopping Atrium:

> Now that's a reason to get up in the morning!
> Beautiful men! Beautiful women!
> Ah, the Atrium. Riding the escalators every day.
> Up and down!
> Too glorious!

Bad ads set up false expectations, lead to disap-
pointment and rage. That is bad customer service.

B. Altman's, a store that catered to sweet old ladies,
once ran a "fashion" ad with copy I didn't understand
then, don't understand now, and never will.

Picture a normal-looking dumb newspaper ad, with a
drawing of a lady wearing a sweater. Nothing else. That's
all. Now read the copy that was published with it:

> If enemy aliens from outer space caused all the knitting
> needles on Mother Earth to disappear into some ultra-sonic
> infundibulum whoosh! like that, 99% of the world's would-
> be best-dressed women would find themselves wearing
> nothing at all this fall.

I rushed to the dictionary to find out what *infundib-
ulum* means: "any of various conical or dilated organs
or parts"! This is a small example of how B. Altman
alienated customers in the days before it went out of
business.

Seven days after the great Mexico City earthquake of
1985, a full-page advertisement appeared in the *Los Angeles Times* for Forest Lawn Mortuary. The headline read:
IF, GOD FORBID, L.A. IS NEXT, OUR COMMITMENT WILL
REMAIN UNSHAKEN.

Another prize goes to Seattle Pacific Industries, which test-marketed a television ad in Los Angeles for its Union Bay Clothing line. The ad showed two teenage boys about to engage in a game of chicken similar to the one made famous in the James Dean movie *Rebel Without a Cause*. Just as in the film, one of the boys drives his car over the cliff. The final shot in this ad shows his clothing floating in the water and the words UNION BAY CLOTHING. FASHION MADE TO LAST.

You can hear "It's not my department" a thousand different ways before you ever get to make a purchase. You can spend an hour in line at the bank or driving around looking for a parking place at the mall.

At Metro Center, an enormous shopping complex in Phoenix, there is a Broadway Department Store. In front of the entrance I once found a parking space that was protected by a brightly colored, striped canvas awning that was supported on brass poles and looked like a miniature circus tent. Under it crouched a Jaguar XKE.

When I got close I saw there was an engraved plaque that said, NO PARKING! THIS SPACE RESERVED FOR STEPHEN P. MEARA II, CHAIRMAN OF THE BROADWAY. I can't imagine why anyone could expect good service out of The Broadway when the boss is exalted and the customer can park over in the satellite B lot where you get out of your car and step in bad drainage or a sea of filth, or where, after you get no more than fifteen steps from your car, your car radio is stolen.

Doesn't it lift your heart when you show up at the front door of the store and signs greet you saying, NO FOOD, NO DRINKS, NO TANK TOPS, NO EXCHANGES, NO RETURNS, NO STROLLERS, NO BARE FEET, NO SMOKING or NO SHIRT, NO SHOES, NO SERVICE?

Welcome to the store!

Bad signs are any signs that depress the customer. Bad signs are bad service.

Littman's Jewelers, a chain of jewelry stores, has a professionally lettered sign that sits on a table in the front of its stores that reads: PLEASE FEEL FREE TO ENJOY YOUR FOOD OR DRINK IN OUR STORE. Why not? If somebody makes a mess in your store, it's because you had a potential *customer* come in!

Bad beginnings are bad service.

LIFE ON HOLD

In the world of customer abuse, everyone hates the telephone. Every service encounter conducted on the telephone is blind; you cannot see your adversary, and you can be eliminated any time they want to put you on hold. Customer frustration is greater on the telephone than it is with ads and bad directions, and almost as great as when the customer is face to face with another human being who doesn't give a damn.

I hate those telephone systems that make you listen to long recorded messages and punch in a series of numbers to finally reach a human being when all you want to know is what time the store closes on Thursdays. If you've dealt with the company before, maybe you *do* know the extension you want. But if you're a new customer, it gets pretty frustrating. If you don't have a Touch-Tone phone, or you are intimidated by these machines and don't understand how they work, you have to sit there and listen to five minutes of recorded drivel before a live human being finally comes on the line.

Metro-North provides commuter rail service between Manhattan and the northern suburbs. It uses one of these automated telephone systems. The recorded voice tells you to press the first four letters of the rail line you want to take. But maybe you don't know that there is a Harlem division or a New Haven line. It tells you to press the first four letters of the station you want to go to. Maybe you want to go to Stamford but you'd go to Greenwich, which is nearby, if there was an earlier train.

Try calling Sears, which uses these automated systems in its New York–area stores. You want to find out about vacuum-cleaner bags. Is it hardware—"press four now"—or appliances and home furnishings—"press five now"? By the time you reason it out in your mind, the recorded voice is telling you about the credit department and catalog pickup. It's maddening. It's a technical defense to the challenging problem of relationships with customers. The driving force is efficiency and the answer they come up with is a system that actually makes it more difficult for the customer to do business with them.

Abuse-by-telephone is having to listen, whether you want to or not, to a recording of Rimsky-Korsakov's "The Flight of the Bumble Bee" for forty-five minutes after a voice—which is not a voice but a recording—tells you, "Thank you very much for calling Woo-Woo Enterprises."

Being on hold is insulting. How much of your life do you want to spend being on hold? When someone asks me, "Will you hold?" I say, "No!" Most of the time the person immediately responds, "Oh, how can I help you?" and I get put through. "All of our agents are presently occupied serving other customers" is also an insult.

If I have to be on hold, I would rather be doing something productive while I cradle the receiver, and it is very hard to write a novel or read a recipe while I'm listening to Frank Sinatra or Charo. Why do I have to listen to elevator music just because someone else happens to like it? If you have to put me on hold, can the cancan.

High-tech telephone systems are as bad as postage meters. They both eliminate the human element. High-tech telephone systems have eliminated the good old operator, but they have passed the job of traffic director right on to you the customer. Postage meters are faster than stamps, but they're ugly and impersonal. True, customers have learned to appreciate automatic tellers better than the people who used to snarl at them from inside their cages at the bank, but they would get out of their cars and march right back inside if they thought there was even a chance that they'd be recognized and greeted by a genuine human being giving fast, efficient, personal service while handling their money.

Once you've penetrated the high-tech interference, the abuse shifts to human form. "I'll see if he's in." Doesn't he or she know if he's in or not? I get the feeling that this secretary is going to put on a backpack and a pair of hiking boots, get out a compass, call out the dogs and sled, and go and find this individual down in the cafeteria. I think it's cheap. It's not good service.

There also has to be another way of saying, "What's this in reference to?" If I wanted to tell a stranger how many jobs I've had, I would do so.

Bonwit Teller tried to break the high-tech habit once. Every person answering a phone at Bonwit was required to say, "Bonwit Teller. Have a nice day." But because most of these people worked in New York, where the phones were busy all the time and people tended to be impatient and unpleasant, it usually came out as kind of a garbled hostile snarl: "BONWITTELLERHAVEANICEDAY—*HOLD!*"

One of the best business telephone greetings I have ever encountered was at Stew Leonard's, the grocery store in Norwalk, Connecticut, which has become a legend of great customer service. There is a woman who almost always answers the phone, a real live human being, and she says simply, "Stew Leonard's. This is Jodie speaking." A real person with a real name.

The first time I ever called, I asked her if I could speak to Stew Leonard. "Sure!" she said . . . and the next voice I heard was his.

FACE TO FACE WITH SERVICE

Most department stores and government offices should have Dante's inscription over the gate of Hell posted above their own doors as a warning to customers:

"ABANDON HOPE, ALL YE WHO ENTER HERE"

Well, congratulations. Now you have made it through the bad ads, impenetrable phone systems, misleading signage, filthy parking lots, and outdated store directories, and are about to come face to face with customer service in the form of a living person.

Disneyland's front door usually creates a highly un-usual impression. When you (and several hundred others) arrive at the park before it opens, you all have to stand there patiently in front of the entrance. But you can watch while a live band lines up until you hear a loudspeaker announcement which says, "Welcome to the happiest place on earth!"—and at the same moment, the gates swing open, the crowd rushes into the park, and the band plays the *William Tell* Overture. The day begins with everyone laughing and relaxed.

The entire Disney empire depends on details like this. Always remember: no detail is small.

But the first moments face to face in most establish-ments are not like those in Disneyland. The first moment is the moment in every business, millions of times each day, when the customer and the service provider meet face to face. You are looking at your lawyer and your lawyer is looking at you. You are looking at your book-keeper, or the policeman, the teacher, or the saleswoman on the third floor at Bergdorf Goodman. You are about to experience service. Who is in charge? Whose money is it, anyway? Who's helping whom? What are your chances that some time during this exchange, you're going to hear that great phrase, "It's not my department"?

Service providers love that phrase. Every time they utter it, it enables them to do less and serve you less.

This is going to be your responsibility.

Sometimes you don't even get to meet the person who is there to serve you face to face. They could be crumpled up on the floor behind their workstation. This actually happened. I was passing by the entrance of the beauty salon at Woodward's in Vancouver. I heard a soft, re-signed moaning and went over to have a look. The clerk was sitting on the floor. I asked her what was wrong and she replied, sincerely, "I just can't take it anymore."

I suppose she was referring to her job, which was

serving customers. I admired her candor, tried to visualize the entity who had hired her in the first place and had then moved coldly on, abandoning her to the misery of her job. She may still be there, or someone may have come along and saved her.

I was in a mall in the Midwest where a girl sat perched on a stool next to a cart, selling handicrafts. She sat there holding her little hands out in front of her.

I started looking through the crafts when she said, "Stop! I can't take your money!" I hadn't even thought about giving her any, but I asked, "Why not?" She showed me her fingernails and announced, "My nails aren't dry!"

I went face to face as fast as possible when Bloomingdale's presented "Japan"—a mammoth merchandising festival of entertainment and goods from Japan. This kind of event is what makes Bloomingdale's Bloomingdale's—merchandise you've never seen before, presented in extremely imaginative surroundings, and all for sale. The promotion is the result of eighteen months of research, two hundred buyer trips to Japan, and a year and a half of graphic and visual planning and execution, culminating in the October weeks when other stores do nothing, waiting for Christmas. So the mobs crowd in to Bloomingdale's to gasp and shiver with delight, and, theoretically, buy something.

I went on a Sunday. I was dazzled a dozen times, but the sin of envy didn't hit me until I saw six fantastic black iron bowls. I wanted them. I needed them. I was going to have them. But first, I had to buy them.

With high anticipation, I informed a salesperson I wanted to buy these bowls.

"You can't," she said. "That set is on display."

"Okay," I said. "I'll buy a set that isn't on display."
I always presume the purpose of display is to sell things, but I am often wrong.

"You can't," she said. "That's the only set we have."

"Call the branches," I said.

"Can't call the branches," she said. "This is Sunday and we're short-staffed."

"Call a manager," I said.

An erect figure wearing a white carnation and no facial expression approached.

"Miss Markoff tells me you are having a problem," he uttered.

"Yes," I said. "I am having a problem. I'm trying to buy something. I'm failing. I want these bowls. I'm told I can't have these bowls because these bowls are on display. There are no more bowls here. We can't call the branches because we're understaffed. I shouldn't have come on Sunday. I can't buy what I want, and all this time I thought the purpose of this store was supposed to be to sell merchandise."

"You got it," he said. "And if you don't like it here, why don't you go shop at Macy's?"

THE RUDENESS SWEEPSTAKES

Can you top any one of these in the Rudeness Sweepstakes?

A clerk behind bars in a post office in Clayton, Missouri, gave me her opinion when I asked to buy stamps

6 1

that were "special, commemorative, unusual, or beautiful": "Honey, they're all ugly to me."

I went into a card shop in the Beverly Center in Beverly Hills and asked a clerk, "Where are the cards for Jewish New Year?" She said, "Why don't you look under *J*?"

A man was bringing down the riot gate in front of a store in a mall at twenty minutes to nine. I asked him, "What time do you close?" He said, "Nine o'clock." I said, "But it's only twenty minutes to nine." He responded, "Let's just say it's nine o'clock as far as you're concerned."

I asked for Kleenex in Kroger's. Someone low down, stocking shelves, didn't even look up, but said, "Nine."

One day on the main floor at Dayton's in Minneapolis I overheard a salesperson with vast experience talking to a customer who was trying to return a pair of panty hose. The clerk reached into the bag, and pulled out a pair of panty hose. She looked not so much at them as through them. The garment was in tatters, perhaps the remnant of some profound personal experience. The saleswoman drew herself up to tower over the customer, and let her have it: "Honey, if you'd cut your toenails, that wouldn't happen."

I went into an absolutely empty food place once that had a hand-lettered sign on the counter which read, IF YOU WANT SERVICE, RING THE BELL *ONCE*!!!

Another place I wandered into had a sign that said, IF YOU NEED ME, HOLLER, I'M IN THE BACK.

I was visiting a mall in Connecticut and stood at the sale table in front of The Gap store while the sole living inhabitant relentlessly drove a vacuum cleaner back and forth in the rear of the store, without so much as a glance to see if another living being had come in. I decided to try an experiment. I picked up eleven identical pairs of pants from the sale table and walked off with them. I carried those eleven pairs of pants through the mall for forty-five minutes, no shopping bag, price tags hanging off them, security buttons still attached, and nobody stopped me or even gave me a second glance.

I decided to go back to The Gap to see if anyone had panicked. Someone had noticed the hole in the sale table and had filled it with eleven more pairs of pants.

Later that afternoon, when The Gap manager was present in my seminar of about three hundred people at the mall, I used the pants as a prop and then returned them to him. He hadn't even been aware that they had been stolen.

It drives me crazy when clerks are talking with their friends on the phone while serving a customer at the same time. Or when the clerk who is taking care of you is talking to another clerk about who got her veins done or Val's latest psychotic episode on *Knots Landing*.

But being off the phone and ready to help customers doesn't guarantee much either. In Muse's, a menswear store in Atlanta, I found two clerks sitting down visiting together (they should have been fired). One called out to me without moving a muscle, "Can I help you?" I said, "No." There was a pause and then he said, "Good!"

I went out once to find a new pair of black shoes. I'm fussy: I went to ten stores in New York one day and I couldn't find anything I liked. The problem was partly that there weren't any interesting shoes. But more importantly I couldn't find any*body* I liked. None of the salesclerks showed even a flicker of interest in me or what I wanted. I'm talking about $400 shoes. No one got up. They were sitting around smoking Gauloises and exhaling Madison Avenue attitude. Nobody took my name; nobody wrote down what I wanted. In one store the fall shoes had not come in yet and the clerk said distractedly, "Why don't you call up in a couple of weeks?" The store looked like it hadn't had a customer in four years. Why should I call *them*? They should call *me*, write to *me*, find *me*, the minute they get a new shipment of black shoes.

A very bored-looking lady with her elbows propped on the counter presided behind a locked jewelry case at Bonwit Teller. I was glancing into the case when she said, "If you see anything you want, let me know. I'll get the key," as though the key were in a bank across town.

The laziest greeting I ever heard was when I walked into a store where a woman in the couture department said to me with this heavy-lidded look of boredom, "Something?"

Can you top these stories? Write and tell me. I want to know. I want to tell everybody else about it too. I want to shout it from the housetops until people realize this is neither right nor necessary. It's just tolerated.

"BEGIN PROBING FOR WANTS AND NEEDS"

If we survive the initial face-to-face encounter, we may actually begin to experience service. Service in action occurs when the customer and the provider, together, engage in the innermost ritual of their relationship. The customer is searching for service; the provider is there to give it. The secretary and the messenger are having a human interchange. The lady in the teller's cage is looking at you with loathing. But you're both still there. And now you are about to be the victim of all their training.

Here are some excerpts from the dearest little training manual in the World. It was published in 1898 by Hess Brothers in Allentown, Pennsylvania. It is simpler and clearer than most of the twenty-volume extravaganzas produced today. The manual was written by "O. N. Powell" and published for Hess employees, many of whom still keep copies in their desks. Here are some quotes from it:

Don't manicure your nails during business hours.

Don't allow a customer to look in vain for somebody to wait upon her while you are engaged in talking to your fellow clerk about last evening's experiences.

Don't be disloyal to your employer.

Don't indulge in gossip.

Don't be discourteous to customers. It's a fault which cannot be excused.

Don't stand in a listless manner while customers are examining goods—be attentive, and show an interest in your employer's business.

Don't argue or contend with business associates in the presence of customers.

Don't say "I was not hired to do that." It might cost you your situation and reference to obtain another.

Don't be afraid of making suggestions for the betterment

of the business. If heard from[,] it is a sign that you are using your eyes and ears to advantage.

Don't tell customers that goods on display in windows are not for sale.

Companies spend huge sums of money training people and they still manage to produce ignorant, uncaring help. The fact that a company makes a commitment to providing good customer service doesn't guarantee a thing. It may be a complete waste of time. One look at the training materials and you can see why.

A national chain of retail stores selling home-improvement and decorating products put together an enormous set of manuals for its new employees. Some of the material was basic and concerned itself with how to calculate commissions on sales or admonished salesclerks to "load all the merchandise into the customer's car quickly and courteously." A big part of it dealt with customers: how to approach them, how to speak to them, how to get them into the store. Many sample dialogues are so ridiculous that I laugh out loud when I read them. The employees must, too. This is from a section on telephone approaches and greetings:

SALESPERSON: Thank you for calling Woo-Woo, the home improvement experts. This is Chuck, how may I help you?

CUSTOMER: Chuck, this is Pete Wilson. I was wondering, do you sell air nailers?

SALESPERSON: Air nailers, Pete? I'm not familiar with air nailers. What do you use them for?

CUSTOMER: Oh, it's a pneumatic tool you use for framing a house.

SALESPERSON: Oh, I understand. No, we do not sell pneumatic tools, but tell me Peter, are you in the construction business?

CUSTOMER: Oh, no, I'm building my own home, with the help of my father.

SALESPERSON: Your own home! That's great. Have you ever built a home before?

These sitcom extravaganzas go on for pages and pages with admonishments in the margins to the salesperson to "Talk forcefully; be enthusiastic," and, best of all, "Begin probing for wants and needs."

Every company in retailing has someone called a training manager who writes this stuff. In retailing this is often considered to be a second-rate job. It is often someone who first has failed as a merchant. These people teach theory: "Always display a cheerful attitude"; "There are five steps in every sale." The five steps are: approach the customer, determine the customer's need, present the merchandise, close the sale, and thank the customer.

To come up with those five steps of every sale takes most companies several years of weeping and agonizing and research, and then they write a whole chapter and produce videos about every one of them.

All these things are true. It's just that they don't work.

PARROT SERVICE

The problem with training courses is that they do not treat either the customer or the provider as individuals.

Instead, they propose formula "answers." Most retail stores, for instance, spend years sweating out techniques for "customer approach." They worry about "Can I help you?" versus "May I help you?" as if it mattered. Or they preach about "the merchandise approach." That means the victims of these courses are condemned to stand in their departments asking nonsense questions like, "Isn't this a lovely Thermos?" or "I notice you looking at that flannel shirt."

The Woo-Woo manual also has a list of the different approaches to a customer. There is also the Personal Approach, the Service Approach, and, my favorite, the Acknowledgment Approach—to be used when you are busy with one customer and another comes into the store with no other salesperson available. Then you are to "politely excuse yourself for a moment with your first customer, explaining, 'At Woo-Woo we like to welcome personally each of our customers to our store. Excuse me for a moment while I welcome that shopper. I'll be right back.' "

This manual probably cost $100,000 to produce and is full of inflated advice like, "Practice good habits. Try to maintain a healthy body," "Stand erect," and "Don't overdress." Employees are insulted by this kind of stuff, and it reflects in how they behave with the public. Mechanical stimulus worked for Pavlov: he trained dogs to salivate every time he rang a bell. It doesn't work as well with customers.

Every customer is created separate and individual, and every person providing service should be, too. But they're not. Wouldn't it be wonderful if the people who serve were encouraged to be themselves? But instead we love groups and group response. "Do not think. Just listen and repeat after me." If you have people all saying the same three or four syllables, they're not thinking. It really is conformity and I don't think great management or great service has *anything* to do with conformity.

I believe in managing individuals, even if you have three hundred thousand employees at Chrysler. There are as many different answers as there are customers. It is far more important to get people to *think for themselves* than to "repeat after me."

Restaurants specialize in mechanical, memorized service. They train their service people in the art of artificial cheerfulness. It all starts when they bounce right up to your table, fix you with a semi-conspiratorial eye, and hit you with "Can I getcha something from the bar (*heh, heh*)?" It's as though only the waiter and you will ever know the depth of your excesses. The real attack begins after you have your "something from the bar," and it's time for him to belly up to your table, all flashing teeth and promises, and begin his avalanche of unsolicited information.

"Hi there, my name is Rud"—or Beth or Jim or Brad—"and it is my pleasure to be your waiter tonight. In addition to everything on the menu, there are some specials the chef has prepared . . ." And here beginneth the longest descriptions of the most tortured dishes you can imagine.

Everything is *nice*—"nice piece of veal," "really nice lobster bisque"—and everything is "on a bed of" or "stuffed with" or "accompanied by." This is not service. It is verbal anesthesia.

After two minutes of this relentless attack, you lapse into the same fixed stare you use while watching caged birds hop and nod and bob up and down. And little Rud just bobs and bubbles along, just like a budgie in a bird cage, chirping cheerfully about how nice it all is and how it comes on a bed of . . .

When he stops or gasps for breath, you realize you

have not retained a word he has said and you probably order something, anything, mainly to stop his chirping.

But by the fourth time he comes back to ask, "Is everything all right?" you may have to restrain yourself from standing up and shouting, "No, little Rud, everything is not all right and the most not-all-right thing about this whole experience is you! Stop bobbing up and down. If we wanted to spend the night with a bird, we would eat at the zoo. And stop repeating yourself. Take a risk. Make something up. Say something spontaneous. Think more of yourself. Think more of us. Oh, hell, we're not here to train you, and you don't care enough about yourself to train yourself. Bring us the check. Don't even think of telling us what a pleasure it's been to be our waiter tonight. If you don't mean it, don't do it."

Mechanical trainers exist all over the place. There is a hotel chain that makes every telephone operator say to every guest request, "It is my pleasure to connect you." Sickening.

If only they knew the simplest secret of selling and serving customers:

Find out what they want,

and how they want it,

and give it to 'em,

just that way!

So to begin, there is only *one* way; to talk to customers about the thing they are most interested in: themselves. And that means it will be *different* with each customer.

This is why all training manuals and all formulas for "How to Approach the Customer" are useless. There is no one right way to approach the customer; there are as many different ways as the number of people who ever stand before you.

Every customer is an individual and so is every service person. And there's the answer: all those "steps" (greeting, approach, determine needs, suggest, etc., etc., etc.) are right, but none of the answers ever are.

Why don't those companies that teach the parrot approach just fire everyone and hire a horde of parrots? Parrots are easily trained and they never worry about their individuality. These parrots could just hang there, chained to their perches, perpetually squawking, "Can I help you? Can I help you?" with just as much effect as most salespeople.

Mechanical service is bad service.

LIP SERVICE

Lip service is even worse than mechanical service. And we are having an epidemic. Suddenly service providers are starting to issue guarantees and pay their customers after providing them with bad service. The Marriott Hotels say that if your breakfast is delivered more than fifteen minutes late, it's free. The pizza place offers a discount if your order is not delivered within thirty minutes. The restaurant provides free desserts if entrées don't come in ten minutes, and the bank hands out five-dollar bills if customers wait in line more than five minutes.

This automatically gives all the employees permission to deliver your breakfast and your pizza late; free desserts are figured into the selling cost of the restaurant's shoddy operations and charged to the customer; and banks can now plan on keeping customers waiting in lines forever, as long as they come around afterwards and give them some money for their time.

Banks are the worst.

A third of the customers surveyed by the trade paper *American Banker* in 1989 had a complaint about bad service, and half of those closed their accounts because of it. The two prime reasons customers give for changing banks are moving and bad service. Bad service includes errors and inaccuracy, inefficiency, slow response, and lines that are just too long. (You will wait in line ninety minutes a week. That's 4,680 minutes, or 78 hours per year. The average U.S. life expectancy is 74.9 years. You will wait in line 5,842 hours during your lifetime, just slightly less than a *year*. You'd better bring a good book to read.)

So, bank marketing people are perfecting the art of apology and calling it customer service. In 1985 the Key Bank of Wyoming pioneered a "no-goof guarantee" offering five dollars if anyone caught the bank in a mistake. Wells Fargo has a "Five Minute Max" promotion. Customers are handed one dollar at Glendale's Fidelity Savings if tellers don't greet them by name, and smile and thank them.

And try to understand the labyrinthine complexities of Empire of America's "guarantees." The customer gets five dollars if employees are discourteous (whatever that means), a new telephone if the customer's call isn't answered in four rings, a coffee mug if the wait for service exceeds ten minutes, one-quarter percent off the rate of interest charged if a loan application isn't answered the same day—and *more*.

This is complicated, costly, insulting, and would be completely unnecessary if the bank did its job right instead of double-stunning customers with awful service and incentives.

There is nothing wrong with genuine guarantees—they inspire confidence. They can even help to forge better products and service by communicating with customers.

Here, in chiseled English, is a request to customers added to the five-year guarantee offered by Broadaker, Ltd., an English company that makes Pivotelli storage equipment.

It is our policy to constantly review the specifications of our products and update them in light of any design improvements and changes in technology. Our customers provide an excellent information source on which this constant product evaluation can take place. We would ask you in this connection to complete the questionnaire below, although this is not obligatory and in no way affects the validity of the guarantee.

Would you rather read and respond to that, or have the folks at Broadaker send you five dollars because the product they sold you did not function?

Nowadays, if you make the "C" sign, you can receive free phone calls from AT&T, free repairs from Amoco, no charge if a room at a Hampton Inn fails to meet customer standards of cleanliness, comfort, or safety, free temporary help from Manpower if service is not satisfactory, a free trip to the Los Angeles airport if the airport shuttle bus fails to pick up passengers within fifteen minutes of the scheduled time, and you can even return a 1990 Oldsmobile to the dealer, unconditionally.

And, you can have all this *instead* of the service you were willing to pay for in the first place! This is not service. This is lip service. It is no substitute for genuine customer service. It costs the providers a lot of time and money. It does not really satisfy customers. It is a shame.

We are perfecting our apologies instead of our service. Wouldn't it be revolutionary if banks and pizza places and restaurants and room service just provided good service when you wanted it?

It is true that good service means never having to say you're sorry.

HOW TOO MUCH CHANGE KILLS CUSTOMER SERVICE

Customers thrive on change, and they require it. They rush to see autumn leaves, and they eat at the Four Seasons, which costs a lot of money but promises not only consistent excellence in food and service, but also a complete seasonal change in uniforms, plates, and tablecloths. *And* they change the trees and flowers and of course they present new food.

Everybody agrees that American Airlines serves terrific hot fudge sundaes. But that was yesterday. The next time the same hot fudge sundae comes out, it's just as good, but no longer new. And one of these days American Airlines' customers will grumble, "I wish they'd take this tired ice cream off their menu." The passenger who commutes every week between the coasts soon begins to suffer from hot fudge sundae glut.

But it is dangerous and unwise to change the attitude and execution of customer service.

Companies that manage service the best are those that develop a policy and then stick to it. This is very difficult in an age of mergers, acquisitions, and brand new management every week.

It paralyzes middle managers and dumbfounds customers to find that whatever was true last week is not true now, and might change again after Friday. When this happens often enough, employees who work there tend to go into "hold" and do nothing.

I've seen it myself when I look into the faces of an audience that is sitting there being astounded by my socks or by something I am saying, and so many of them give me a clear facial expression signifying as they watch me, "This, too, shall pass."

Too much change happened a few years ago at Eaton's, the Canadian department store. They decided to create a single central buying office in Toronto and dissolved the regional offices, along with their associated people, all across the country. This was very economical. This way they could have far fewer buyers, and buy more thousands of hammers at better prices, put them in a central warehouse, and send them out to stores which would be required to sell them whether they wanted to or not. It was, at least, a clear plan.

But they didn't stick with it. They got a new manager who decided he wanted to restore regional differences and that the customers in Calgary, Alberta, don't want the same merchandise as the people in Halifax, Nova Scotia. So they decentralized the buying operation and hired lots of buyers to establish offices in different regions.

Now they could buy merchandise that would serve customers better in different parts of the country. It took about five years to get this running smoothly. But then, someone decided that it was time to cut costs. They refired the buyers and recentralized the buying in Toronto. The company changed from serving customers to serving itself, and all these changes almost caused people to stop working entirely, because now they were certain that nothing would ever last.

When employees get mixed or messy messages from their management, the customer suffers. And nobody has had more varieties of management than Eastern Airlines. Their flights were late, their maintenance was criticized, and they had the rudest employees in all of aviation. The last clever thing they did was to invent the shuttle—and that was over twenty years ago.

When Donald Trump bought the foul and nearly bankrupt Eastern Airlines Shuttle, the first things he did were change the name to the Trump Shuttle, repaint the planes, and put in better seats and toilets.

But he also notified the leftover, demotivated Eastern employees that their most important job was to provide outstanding customer service. He bought the women employees each a set of good pearl earrings and a necklace, and told them to wear them. He motivated his staff through generosity, taste, and a clear-cut order.

TALES OF DISASTER

This probably did more to improve service on the "new" shuttle faster than ten full-page ads in East Coast newspapers and a ten-years-in-the-making training manual. The shuttle, which had become a money-losing, hated necessity to many thousands of travelers, with the same planes and schedules and prices, became profitable almost immediately and won back the loyalty of travelers who had become exhausted.

Then, on the Trump Shuttle's first Thanksgiving Day, he offered low, low $45 fares to passengers who showed up at the terminal with a can of food to donate. In this way the shuttle and its passengers together provided another kind of service to homeless people who had no place to spend the holiday.

Now passengers must choose between competing shuttle services: Trump and Pan Am. The outcome will be based entirely on service and consistency.

I flew Eastern from New York to San Juan once, and the flight attendant, who had for some unknown reason decided to be pleasant to me, said with a sneer, "How'd you get on the pig flight?"

"What's the pig flight?" I asked.

"Any flight that goes to San Juan."

He thought that was very funny and proceeded to share with me stories about women giving birth in the back of the plane and bringing live chickens on board under their skirts.

These people are usually called *passengers*. But not at Eastern.

The meal was also terrible. I was served something that was supposed to be meat loaf. I took it out of the dish, dried it out, and sent it back to Frank Borman, Eastern's president at the time, along with a letter asking if he would ever eat anything like this. Twelve years later I am still waiting for an answer.

CHANGE KILLS CUSTOMER SERVICE

Writing letters makes it easy on the bad service provider. All they have to do is throw it away.

I was beaten up by three crack addicts around the corner from where I live in New York. After I recovered, I made a massive effort to demand the services I pay taxes for by writing, and getting others to write, a grand total of seven thousand letters to the mayor, local officials, senators, congressmen, and others, including the President of the United States.

I was an outraged and battered "customer" and I was making seven thousand frantic "C" signs. Every letter contained a photocopy of my hideously swollen face and a detailed description of the event.

I received *one* answer.

It was from then Vice President George Bush and it was a form letter. It was, in a sense, more insulting, and certainly less believable than the 6,999 answers I did not receive.

> The Vice-President has asked that I send his thanks for your recent letter and the thoughts you expressed [my hideous deformed photograph and near death!]. He is pleased to have your comments and is sharing them with members of his staff. You can be sure he will keep them in mind as he moves forward with the work of the transition.

Want a translation? "It's not my department"—write me when something important happens.

The beating had taken place at Madison Avenue and 36th Street in New York. When it was over, I dragged myself two blocks home and called the police before going to the emergency room at New York University Hospital. "Sorry," the police said, "you've called the wrong precinct. The crime took place on the *other* side of Madison Avenue." It wasn't their department.

TALES OF DISASTER

What message do most companies communicate to their employees about customer service? Sometimes none, and often a confusing or ambiguous one. It's usually an afterthought relegated to personnel, a department that operates on rules and tests and job specifications and employee identification cards instead of customers. At most department stores, employees are taught that the most important thing in their job is to stock the shelves well, keep it neat, and ring it up right. After that, they're on their own.

Don Katz, author of *The Big Store*, a detailed book about the history of and crisis at Sears, told me that during the late 1970's and early 1980's Sears, like most retailers, fought a kind of civil war about service, between their operating costs and what they referred to as the "teenybopper question." Sears gave up its long-standing tradition of putting only informed and dedicated sales help on the floor. They decided to let these people retire, replacing them with much cheaper youngsters at minimum wage who had had little training.

Under the old system, people worked for Sears almost their entire lives. "As they grew up the company moved them 17 to 23 times within a 25 to 30 year career," Katz said. "Whole families were moved from town to town. Part of it was a sense of service to the people. This was a company that actually provided something of value to people and they actually would get back a lot at the store level because people were amazingly loyal." Even now, as crippled as Sears is, the public still thinks of it in the top five stores for trustworthiness and quality. It's amazing because the reality hasn't kept up with the image at all.

"WE JUST CAN'T GET GOOD HELP"

Sometimes it helps to go to a manager if your service provider isn't giving you what you want.

And sometimes it doesn't.

I travel a lot, and after I survive taxis and airlines and porters and lost luggage and registration lines, I have to sleep in hotels. Service is pretty good at the Bel Air in Los Angeles or the Carlyle in New York, which is fine if you have $400 a night for a room with bath. (That's about $50 an hour, so enjoy it.)

But most hotels aren't like that.

The worst hotel experience I can remember was at a Hyatt in Cherry Hill, New Jersey. In my first room, the plastic shower curtain reeked of curdled mold. This was a room on the "concierge floor" of a Hyatt, but there was no bathtub. I like to take baths. The rug was filthy, and acoustical tiles were missing from the ceiling. I made a list of about forty things that were wrong with this room and I called down to the desk.

"I would like to change my room."

"There aren't any other rooms," the desk clerk said. "We're full."

I said, "Come up and just look at this room."

I finally got them to move me—twice. I was in my third room on a floor that was being redone, with sawdust everywhere—when the manager showed up and said, "I hear there is a problem."

"Yeah," I said, now peeved and feisty, "and it is your fault because all these people work for you."

"There's just no need to talk like that," he said.

"Let me take you on a tour of your hotel," I said, which is something I think a customer should do. So we went, and when it was all finished the manager said to me, "Well, you know, this hotel is probably so bad it shouldn't be part of the Hyatt chain. We just can't get good help. We are in southern Jersey. I wish I could do something for you."

This snively Dickens character tried to ingratiate himself with me but did not try to fix the problem. Finally he said, "Do you mind if I send you a little gift?"

"I'd rather have a good room," I said, "but since you don't have any, why don't you send me a little gift?" He sent me a catering department "party platter" with enough cubed morsels of cheese on toothpicks to satisfy a small convention. It was served without a knife or fork or anything to drink, and was tied up in cheap yellow cellophane with his compliments. I ran into him later and said, "We're bringing four hundred people in here tomorrow from the Cherry Hill Mall, and I am making a speech. Why don't you come? It's about excellence."

"I don't know what that mall has to be so hot about," he said. "They don't have good service either."

There was formerly a Holiday Inn in Quincy, Illinois, that once put me in a room a long distance from the front desk. Everything was "very nice" until I suddenly woke up, in the dark, in the middle of the night, and sensed most peculiar movements in my room. I switched on the light and screamed. The entire ceiling was covered with cockroaches. The light had startled them and they were swarming. I called the front desk and exclaimed that my room was *full* of cockroaches.

"WE JUST CAN'T GET GOOD HELP"

The man at the desk said wearily, "Yes, I know. That whole wing is full of them."

I was trying to check out of a small, chic, Caribbean hotel but I had been overcharged $380.00 on my bill, and I wasn't going to pay it until they corrected it. The taxi was waiting to take me to the airport. The man behind the desk said he couldn't correct the bill without the manager's approval. "Well, get the manager," I said, and he said to me, "You'll have to wait. The manager is in the ocean. We cannot disturb him. Every day at five o'clock the manager goes for a swim!"

The Ritz-Carlton in Laguna Niguel is not a budget hotel. For $250 per day or more they promise their guests fine service, and most of the time they provide it. But at this level of promise and expectation they should deliver it *all* of the time. A group of fifty-two of us stayed there for a meeting, and we were all thrilled by the staff and the service until the very last second.

How sad it was, then, at five-thirty in the morning, when all fifty-two of us stood in the lobby waiting for the bus to take us on the long, long ride to Los Angeles International Airport. We wanted coffee. There was no coffee. There was no room service. There was "no way" anyone could get us coffee. Imagine our attitude as we all stood around watching the staff behind the registration desk drinking coffee they'd made from their own machine.

"I'M MAD AS HELL AND I'M NOT GOING TO TAKE IT ANYMORE"

Sometimes things get bad enough that you lean out the window and scream, "I'm fed up, and I'm not going to take it anymore."

One day ten years ago a machine at my bank made a mistake. It bounced ninety-three of my business checks—a whole month's worth. Suddenly, I had bad credit with ninety-three people I deal with regularly. I rushed right over to the bank to see what they were going to do about it. The branch manager was alarmed and apologetic. (I hate apologies; if things go right you don't ever need them.) He somehow reprocessed all the checks immediately and I went back to my office.

Four days later I found out the same thing had happened again. Ninety-three checks bounced a second time.

I roared back to the bank and attacked the manager. He didn't even know this had happened. I told him he had run out of excuses and that we needed to fix this disaster *now*. The manager whined. He blamed the machine, and the system, and said he didn't know what to do next. And then he said, "I'm only human."

I tend to have psychotic episodes whenever I hear
that remark. It is the last refuge of whiners. Whenever
anyone says "I'm only human," it usually means they
have screwed up badly. "I'm only human" never means
anything great is going on—even though Mozart and
Shakespeare were "only human." I am longing for someone to give me splendid, caring service, and then, just
once, explain it as "only human."

I knew what I wanted: I wanted my creditors paid
instantly and I needed intensive care. I asked the branch
manager where I could find the president. He gave me
the president's name and his address on Wall Street, and
I grabbed my paperwork and jumped into a cab.

Whenever you get into a Manhattan cab, it's a good
idea to be braced for some form of hell. But this taxi had
a surprise in it. On the passenger side of the bulletproof
partition was, I was startled to see, a little sign that said,
"Smile! God loves you!" I thought my luck might be
changing, but I was wrong. "It's not my department"
comes in unexpected places. I leaned forward to praise
the driver. "Hey," I said, "what a great sign!" and the
driver turned back and snarled, "It's not my cab!"

I entered the Wall Street skyscraper prepared to stay
until my customer disaster had been rectified. I walked
onto the fifty-first floor and made my way past ranks of
executive secretaries, vice presidents, assistant vice
presidents, senior vice presidents, and executive vice
presidents (all of whom should have been serving customers) past conference rooms and corporate art and
coffee stations and presented myself to one of the president's executive assistants. Just behind her the president's door was open, and I could see him in there at
his desk, merging and acquiring.

"Appointment?" she gasped. "What's this in reference to?"

"I'm a customer," I said. "I just need a minute of his time and I am going in." She froze. I moved. I was in, making the "C" sign at the president.

When I walked in, I said, "I'm mad as hell and I'm not going to take it anymore!"

The president said, "Good film. Now what can I do for you?"

I told him about the machine's mistakes and the manager's helplessness. I told him I wanted cash delivered, by messenger if necessary, to every office in New York that had been notified not once, but twice, about my "insufficient funds," and money orders wired to every office out of town. I told him I thought it would help if an explanation from the bank accompanied every payment.

"Okay," he said. "I'll take care of it." I was so shocked that I didn't know what to do next. I had expected to be taken from the premises by security guards or given a psychiatric evaluation. It had happened so fast that I wondered why he did it. It may have been to get this noisy person out of his office, but I was satisfied. He had taken the responsibility; he would figure it out.

I had told him what I wanted,

and how I wanted it,

and, bless his heart, he did it for me,

just that way.

Suddenly, I wasn't mad as hell and I didn't have to take it anymore.

TAKING PINE TREES TO CHINA

Bad service can make your best dreams backfire. I had the brainstorm once of taking eight hundred baby pine trees to China. I wanted to put a living tree into the hand of each Chinese executive that I was going over to teach about marketing their products to North America. I thought that the individual personal exchange of this living symbol of our continent would flatter and convince them that they should think of our meeting as a growing experience. Great idea, Peter, great idea.

It was a good thing I had this idea seven months before our trip. First, Canadian customs said "No," and customs in China also said, "No." They said it couldn't be done. I didn't have much support. The sponsors of the trip thought it sounded like a lot of trouble (they were right), and the public relations agency that was supposed to be helping us with all these intricate international negotiations didn't think it was such a great idea (probably because it wasn't their idea). It was "No, No, No," all the way.

I really wanted to hear "Yes." I wheedled and complained and investigated and researched. I arranged to get the trees delivered early enough to put them through their period of quarantine. I processed forms. I persuaded and enthused, and, finally, both Canada and China said "Yes."

We bought eight hundred hardy baby saplings and took them to DHL, the international shipping service, at the Toronto airport, to be tended through customs and sent to China.

Then we went to China. Our first stop was Shanghai. No deliveries. No messages. No trees. Disaster.

It was time to panic. We faxed and telegrammed and telephoned. Panicking, like everything else in China, is extremely difficult. We rushed back to the Shanghai Airport to the DHL office. They got started tracing the trees all the way back to Toronto, but it was a hopeless situation. They soon reported that they were terribly sorry, but it was Friday afternoon and almost six o'clock, and the Shanghai office was closing, and would we call back on Monday?

Our meetings were scheduled for Monday, and by then it would be too late. DHL simply abandoned us and we, therefore, had no choice but to abandon our baby pine trees.

Eventually we learned what had happened to our trees. DHL, the company that advertises its great customer service on television, on radio, and in print—worldwide—had taken our eight hundred trees and shipped them *by mistake* to Argentina.

Even after DHL located them, they did nothing to save either the living trees or our meeting by trying to get them back to us so that we could give them to our people. It was not their department, and DHL was having the last say, and they were saying "No!"

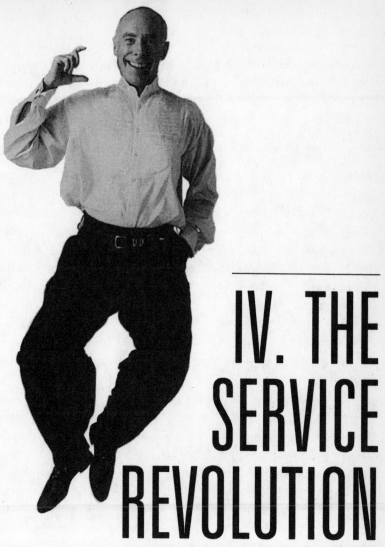

IV. THE SERVICE REVOLUTION

BECOMING A BETTER CUSTOMER

THE MEEK WILL INHERIT NOTHING

"Find out what they like,

And how they like it,

And let 'em have it,

Just that way."

This little verse is sung by two flamboyant Harlem women celebrating their men in the Fats Waller musical *Ain't Misbehavin'*. Nell and Armelia are taking responsibility for making themselves and their boyfriends happy. They think it's entirely *their* department.

If you change the words a little—

Find out what they want,

and how they want it,

and *give* it to 'em,

just that way!

—it could be the philosophy of the oldest profession in the world. In fact, it could be the simplest secret of being a great service provider of any kind.

It could be the revolutionary customer's creed:

Tell 'em what you want,

and how you want it,

and make 'em do it,

just that way!

And it could be the motivating manager's motto.

You are the customer. But you still need to fight. Service is hardly ever automatic. When you're face to face with the college registrar, or a waiter or a clerk or the exterminator, you've got to revolt, demand, persuade, supervise, encourage, reward, and remind the service provider to do what he or she is getting paid for. In order to do all this you've got to be a serious customer: a fighter. You've got to decide to stop tolerating mediocrity, and learn to act continuously as though you were fed up and not going to take it anymore.

Famous retailer Stanley Marcus of Neiman Marcus once set out to prove there is no service. He decided that for a period of one year he would not buy anything unless it was sold to him. In that year, he estimates he saved $45,000.

You have to care. Most American customers don't. They don't care what kind of juice they have for breakfast, which table they sit at, or where they do their banking. They rent videotapes from "the nearest place." The very first step in becoming a great customer is caring about details.

Don't eat at a restaurant without researching it. Walk into the restaurant any afternoon before you reserve a romantic Saturday night, and ask to see the menu. Walk through and decide where you'd like to sit.

You may not think you can "interview" La Côte Basque, but the attitude you get at the time you ask is very likely to be the same attitude you will get later, when you're paying for it. Later, if you have to, you can send the food back, you can reject the wine, ask for a different waiter. But if you make the "C" sign in advance, you won't have to do it later and spoil your Saturday night.

If you are uninformed, you are asking for trouble. The first way to be a great customer is to prove that you know as much or even more about the service you are paying for than the person providing it.

You have to be informed; know what's available. Don't go through life without the yellow pages, airline guides, theater seating charts, maps, guides, and agents. Do not ever enter a hospital without reading a copy of "The Patient's Rights." It is usually available at admissions. If a store has a guarantee policy, read it. Send in the warranty forms on new appliances.

You also have to know when enough is enough. *Network* showed us the spectacle of thousands of angry customers in America leaning out their windows and screaming into the night, "I'm fed up and I'm not going to take it anymore!" Everyone loved the movie—nobody did anything.

Becoming fed up is the starting point at which you begin to become a great customer.

Motorola, the big electronics manufacturer, finally

got fed up with the service it was getting, and the company suddenly started making the "C" sign at hotels, travel agencies, and delivery companies.

Motorola said, in effect, "We are the customer;

This is what we want,

and how we want it,

so give it to us,

just that way."

Motorola issued strict quality standards to these suppliers and promised that if they failed to measure up they would be struck from its list of approved vendors. The survivors would win long-term contracts. Motorola, which spends about $100 million a year on messenger, trucking, and similar services, made the "C" sign—the sign of the customer. As a result of its decision, Motorola winnowed the number of van lines it did business with from seventeen to two, motor carriers from ten to two, and couriers from eight to two. Motorola is a great customer because it defined its goals and stuck to them.

Sam Walton is a fanatical believer in customer service, the chairman of Wal-Mart Stores, and the richest man in America. He stunned the manufacturing establishment with his Green plan: in the fall of 1989 he announced that Wal-Mart would not buy products or packaging that damaged the environment. People have been fretting about this for years, but Sam took action. And when Sam is unhappy, everyone is unhappy. This man, by demanding better customer service, has taken a giant step toward saving the planet, and I, for one, appreciate it and thank him for it!

You are the customer; you can have anything you want, if you are prepared to fight for it. There are 54,000 seats in Busch Stadium; where would you like to sit? A Boeing 727 has 185 seats; if you don't specify what you want, you will be seated in the middle of a row of three.

Airlines offer twenty-four meal choices, but if you are not informed, you eat what everyone else eats and you suffer. Most restaurant and hotel bills make mistakes, and hardly ever in your favor, but since you probably don't think it's nice to read it and question the staff, you pay too much and then you thank them. When they ask if you "enjoyed your stay," you always say, "Yes, it was very nice." So was your rotten meal, the lousy play, and the fact that your doctor kept you waiting two and a half hours while everyone around you coughed and sputtered. Now *you* are coughing, too, because somebody once told you that "patience is a virtue."

There are at least five different ways to get from Santa Fe to Guanajuato, Mexico, and these can take as little as six hours or as much as four days. Your best weapon is information, but you need to work it out with schedules, routing, airplanes, trains, and cars.

You need to search for a doctor, or you can just keep on with your old family friend. You can look at twenty apartments or you can just take the first one the agent shows you. You can act grateful just to get seats behind a pillar for *Phantom of the Opera* or you can make the box office tell you when you can get seats in the fourth row center for any performance within the next six months.

You need to be demanding, precise, persistent, and prepared to put up with the astonished reactions as people learn that you are not kidding. A great customer is a fighter, not a whiner.

Remember this: A great customer knows with absolute certainty that the meek will inherit . . . *nothing!*

GET AN AGENT

An agent is anyone who will fight your customer battles for you. And an agent can often do it better than you can. Even a mediocre travel agent can write a ticket and mail it to you, so you can skip the trauma of ever going into a ticket office. But a great travel agent will get you the best price and a seat by the window and the food you want to eat and will see that you get credit for every flight or hotel reservation on any applicable bonus programs —and a great travel agent costs you, the customer, nothing. Travel agents get paid by the services they are buying for you. But you still have to find and direct a travel agent. Get one who handles *individuals*, not massive groups; you need individual arrangements, not group discounts.

An agent can be your friend at the bank who knows you and can short-cut the lines and procedures that make getting service a trauma. Befriend the nursing supervisor at the hospital so you get your medication on time and the food that you want. Get the name of the clerk on the phone at Lands' End who might remember you when you need an order straightened out, and might even call you back. Find the personal shopper in the department store. You, the customer, must find your own agents everywhere, and make them responsible for your comfort and happiness by telling them

---

What you want,

and how you want it,

and make 'em do it for you,

just that way!

Most hotels have concierges. Try tipping them in advance sometime, telling them how fine you know their service is going to be while you are there. When the concierge says things like, "You can call housekeeping for that," and "I'll give you the number of the health club," you can say, "No, you're the concierge, you do it, and call me back with the answer."

When you check into the hospital, ask to see the Patient Advocate, and tell her or him you want help getting what you are paying for. Tell the Patient Advocate you hate the word *patient*—which is something no customer should ever be—and to call you *customer*.

Continuously strive to perfect your list of agents, but remember, you still have to tell them what to do. A real estate agent in the Napa Valley presumably knows more about real estate in the Napa Valley than you do. But you need to make sure this real estate agent knows about *you* before he or she drives you to the nearest available house and announces, "It's perfect! It's you!" A doctor should know how to amputate your foot better than you do, but it's your foot and you are the customer. Lawyers are better at bickering than you are, but first you have to find one who still listens before she or he begins talking.

Great agents and concierges and Patient Advocates and theater ticket brokers and businesses that deliver are not born, they are made—by informed, aggressive customers.

A good customer is a tough customer. There is a very tough customer in the Bible. God tells Moses, his agent, exactly what he wants, and how he wants it, and he even tells Moses what he will do if the Israelites don't do it just that way.

In Exodus 19, verse 3, God begins with "Thus shalt thou say to the house of Jacob, and tell the children of Israel . . ."

Then follow *sixteen chapters* of detailed instructions.

The people, it seems, do not do it "just that way" the first time. "And the Lord sent a plague upon the people. . . ."

Then God writes it down for Moses: "He wrote upon the tables the words of the covenant, the ten commandments." God wants Moses to be as precise as possible in telling the people what He wants and how He wants it. By now they all know what He will do if they don't do it just that way: He will smite them.

THINGS AN AIRLINE DOESN'T WANT YOU TO KNOW

The worst thing about travel is traveling. The ads promise you an airborne heaven of pampering and delight, with every need anticipated, the objective being to rejuvenate your body and your spirit, while getting you from place to place. But this has hardly ever been known to happen. Arm yourself with information, get an agent, and prepare to battle for your comfort before you leave the house.

Always carry an airline guide. The airlines won't tell you—but this passengers' Bible will—what you can do when your flight is canceled. You should use it to book yourself another flight the moment your flight is "delayed." That way, two hours after your flight is canceled, you'll be first to be traveling on some other flight. Your airline guide will also tell you which other airlines can get you to where you're going. Many tickets are interchangeable within the industry. The airlines hate you to know this; they'd rather have you wait three days to travel with them.

You need to know your rights and all the possibilities. If United Airlines cancels a 747 flight and dumps 385 passengers back into the ugly Sydney Airport, you could,

as I did, find out that there is a Continental flight going
the same way in three hours, and United can put you on
it. The day this happened when I was there, United didn't
tell anyone anything. Instead they merely handed out
free drinks vouchers and told everyone we would be
leaving the day after tomorrow—on United. I did get out
on the Continental flight and got home three hours late
instead of two days late. The other passengers got to see
more of Australia.

Another time our flight from Rome to Nairobi was
canceled (most flights going anywhere from Rome are
canceled), and we were told we weren't going, that we
would have to wait three days. But thanks to our airline
guide, we told them that we *were* going with connections
via Athens, and we got to Nairobi almost on time.

Airlines offer a wide choice of meals, but you don't
get them if you don't ask. TWA provides a seafood
plate, a fruit plate, a club sandwich, an antipasto
salad, a chicken salad, and a mesquite-broiled chicken;
children's meals; meals that are low-carbohydrate, low-
sugar, low-sodium, low-fat, low-cholesterol, or low-
calorie; and vegetarian, kosher, and Muslim meals. All
you must do is ask twenty-four hours in advance. Whether
or not you invest in a phone call is up to you. You are
welcome to digest the worst of airline food, which is
what you get when you dine with the rest of the passive
passengers.

You do not need to stand in line at the ticket counter
if you have a boarding pass; you can go straight to the
gate. Nobody seems to know this and boarding passengers
line up like cattle. If the customers are stupid for not
paying attention, the service people are even more stupid
because they forever let this happen.

You can sit wherever you want on an airplane (or a
train or a bus or a truck, for that matter). But you have

to know where you want to sit, and you have to ask for it. Bulkhead seats are great for babies and hideous for anyone else. Seats in the row by the emergency door have more legroom, and the seat backs in the row in front of them cannot recline.

Read the fine print. Some airlines offer first-class baggage stickers to first-class passengers. The theory is that you wait less because your baggage arrives first— this has sometimes been known to happen—and this can save you forty minutes trapped under fluorescent lights listening to "Strangers in the Night."

Find out about your rights. When there are delays, ask for food vouchers. You will get them.

I got on an airplane once and was mistakenly seated in a smoking area. I told the cabin attendant that I had a reserved ticket for nonsmoking, and she said, "Why don't you go out to the gate and get it changed?" I said, "I'm not going to. You are." She was so shocked that she took the ticket without saying a word and left the airplane and got it changed. She's *supposed* to do that. Most people would have said, "Okay, I'll be right back," and pleaded, "Please don't leave without me."

You may even find an agent on the airplane. This person is called a Flight Service Director and it is said to be this person's entire aim in life to make you happy. The Flight Service Director is your concierge or passenger advocate.

You need to know that any airline will deliver your luggage if it happens to send it to the wrong place. You don't have to go back to the airport to get it. The airline clerks have probably been told by some baggage supervisor, "Let them come back to the airport. It costs us thirty dollars to send a messenger." I don't care if it costs them $9 million. It wouldn't cost them a cent if they did it right in the first place.

KEEP YOUR MINTS OFF MY PILLOW

When you say "Get me a hotel room in Los Angeles," you're being completely irresponsible. Los Angeles is three hours from end to end. What area? How much do you want to pay? Do you want a swimming pool? Health club? What kind of experience do you want? What kind of room? If that's what you want—a room—then shut up and relax. But you're paying for sleeping in the room, living in the room, bathing, watching television, dining in the room, and how you feel in the room, and with a little work you can have an experience instead of a test of survival.

But first you need to care. Most people don't. These people are all called "Honey." You can see the couple Honey and Honey looking haggard in the lobby in the morning. They haven't slept.

Once I overheard this description of their agony. It seemed their room was directly above the garbage dumpsters, where every morning a mob of angry sanitation engineers deafened the world by tossing trash cans at maximum velocity into the dumpsters.

Finally, I interrupted Honey and Honey. "For God's sake, why don't you get your rooms changed?" and Honey and Honey said to me, "Oh, it's okay. *We're only staying a week.*"

Honey and Honey are lousy customers. When you first

check in, check out the situation. Ask, "What kind of room are you giving me?" The clerk will look down at your reservation and say, "It says we're giving you a double." Period. What you need to know is that there are going to be doubles on the parking lot, doubles by the pool, doubles with a mountain view, and doubles with a view of nothing, right over the dumpsters. You could see them all if you wanted to. It depends on how much you care.

After you finally reach the room of your choice, take fifteen minutes to decommercialize it. Clear up all the paper trash and counter cards that advertise the hotel's restaurants and lounges—places that are always called "Thimbles" or "Tulips" or "Spectacles." Take the little table tents that tell you too much about TV schedules and jogging paths, take the notices, warnings, and advice, and put them all in a drawer. Stack up the hotel directories, "in-room" magazines, Bibles, tour guides, and other bits of "infotainment." Now go to work on the "amenities." Unwrap the midget soaps in the hotel logo boxes. You will endure the free shampoo and conditioner, shower cap, shoe rag, dental floss, hand lotion, manicure tools, mouthwash, talcum powder, sewing kit.

Try to pry the Saran Wrap off your drinking glasses, and tear up the paper streamer tied around your toilet seat inscribed with a personal message that says, "This toilet has been sanitized especially for you by your maid, Magdalena. You may wish to leave her a gratuity."

Then rearrange the furniture. Place it exactly where you want, in the way you will enjoy it most. Check the lighting possibilities. Call housekeeping for down pillows. Wash your face. Do two minutes of exercise. Relax. Make yourself at home!

I do all this because I'm happier at home than in hotel rooms, and I want to make the best of a bad thing instead of the worst of a bad thing.

Real service is having your breakfast delivered exactly on time. If it is late, you have to calculate whether to shower before or after it arrives. The television and light bulbs should work without your calling for help. I have spent hours struggling to figure out how stoppers work in hotel bathtub drains.

Real service also assures you that nobody invades your room to inventory your minibar while you are in the shower, that the right laundry comes back on time and undestroyed, that the gym is open when you want to use it, that you can get a cab, and that the operator answers within the first eight rings. Hong Kong hotel housekeepers keep your room tidy at all times, but they do not intrude. They place a small, all-but-invisible broom straw against the door. When the straw falls, they know guests have gone out, and they can rush right in and retidy the room. You should always get your messages and a bathtub plug that you can understand. And I don't keep mints on my pillow at home, so keep your mints off my pillow!

Good service anticipates everything you want, and then gets out of your way.

PROBLEMS IN PARADISE

One day while staying at the Kahala Hilton in Honolulu, a hotel renowned for its "service," we discovered that

the Pro Bowl was being played that afternoon in Honolulu's Aloha Stadium, and we wanted to go. I asked an
assistant manager to get us tickets. "No Way," she said,
in that canceling way assistant managers cultivate. "Sorry."

I gave her the "C" sign and attempted to make her
my agent. "But we really want to go. Why don't you see
if you can find out more about it?"

Two minutes later she came back.

"No," she said. "There aren't any tickets. They're
always sold out weeks in advance and the game is this
afternoon."

We went out to talk to David the doorman, a glam-
orous, 280-pound Samoan wearing a helmet and a white
safari suit, who looked like he was definitely alive. We
told him we really wanted tickets to the Pro Bowl.

Without a pause, he said to us, "How would you like
two seats on the fifty-yard line?"

This exchange took place within yards of the assistant
manager, who was seated at her desk rattling papers and
repeating the word *no* to all who approached. The tickets
were $15 each; we gave David a $20 tip, and went off
to sit front-row-center on the fifty-yard line at the Pro
Bowl. I wrote the hotel manager about his two opposed
employees, but he didn't respond.

I decided I wanted to experience a Hawaiian dream
come true—one Perfect Day in Paradise. Back at the
hotel I found a woman perched behind the travel desk,
and I told her what I wanted. She handed me a bunch
of brochures and said, "Read these. If you find anything
you like, I'll sign you up."

She usually gets away with this because she usually
is faced with hordes of nervous tourists who are perfectly
happy sitting in the depths of air conditioned buses gap-
ing at the landscape through heavily tinted windows. It
would have made her very happy if I had simply handed

her my Visa card and signed up for a tour of the nearest pineapple plantation.

But she wasn't going to get away with this with me. I told her that together she and I were going to find out everything there was to know about airplanes, mules, and helicopters, where they all went and when, and what it was like when they got there. Together, we were going to design and execute one Perfect Day in Paradise.

This was a new concept to her. I could tell because of the way she just sat there and looked at me as though I had unexpectedly started speaking Chinese. I am sure she heard me, and she may even have understood what I said, but she was entirely unprepared for a new thought about her job. She had, no doubt, stopped thinking about her job months or even years before she met me. She probably thought of her job exactly the way she thought of herself—that it was over, that there would be few, if any, more changes.

And now, *this* had happened . . .

In that rare and suspended moment while she and I stared silently at each other, I knew that once again I would need to tell her exactly

---

What I wanted,

and how I wanted it,

and I would have to make her do it for me,

just that way.

I felt as though I should be on her side of the desk and she should be paying me, instead of the other way around. Though this was not a perfect day in her life, I was determined that together we were going to create one in mine.

How often, one wonders, does one have to go through all this?

How often does one want a Perfect Day in Paradise?

The day dawned bright and clear, as they say in the brochures, and precisely on time a long white limo whisked us off to the airport, from which we soared up over the dazzling Pacific to Kauai, landing at Princeville. I had always wanted to see the Na Pali cliffs, and today we were going by helicopter; first to be dropped off and abandoned for a perfect picnic in a valley in Heaven for an hour, then re-collected and flown right into the face of nature deep in the island's great volcano, aslant in all its majesty, and then through Waimea Canyon, up the Na Pali coast, and down to earth again. After that we had one hour left, so we commandeered a taxi to see the north shore beaches, talking all the way about whether we wanted to stay there forever, and then went back to the Princeville airport. We flew back to Honolulu, where, just as the sun was setting, we rushed into the ocean for one last swim.

We were swimming not more than fifty yards from the desk where the same woman still sat indifferently handing out brochures to people who made no demands at all. We had had a Perfect Day and she would be glad we were leaving the next morning.

BEING A POLEMIST

A polemist, according to the dictionary, is "an aggressive controversialist devoted to the refutation of error"—a perfect definition of a great customer.

When you go to a store to get a refund, or when you have to call an insurance company because you think your bills are all wrong, prepare for battle. You'll be encountering service providers who do nothing but deal with problems, and by the time you show up, their attitude has usually petrified. You may need to tell them

What to do,

and how to do it,

and make 'em do it for you,

just that way.

Or, you could be chasing the corrections in your bank balance or trying to exchange a set of queen-size sheets for months and months. The service providers who deal with complaints and mistakes are likely to be the most depressed personifications of service you ever encounter.

Life deals them nothing but trouble, in the form of you.
Often one of the few small joys they have is frustrating
you.

Here you get hit with "It's not my department" at
hurricane force. Here you are *never* talking to the right
person or department; you have to go to the sixth floor,
or mail it to a different address, or wait until he or she
checks with his or her supervisor—and supervisors are
always at lunch, or are professionally charming but not
listening to a word you say.

Beware, above all, of returning anything you bought
which paid the service provider a commission. You will
be tearing the service provider's heart out.

Nothing that goes wrong is ever the fault of the person
you're talking to. It's the fault of the computer, which is
down. It's the fault of the buyer, who is buying in Milan.
It's the fault of the weather, which stopped the service-
man. It's the fault of the lab, which lost your X ray.
Nothing is anybody's department.

Arm yourself with everything: correspondence, re-
ceipts, even tape recordings if you've got them. If you
prepare as if you were going to defend your life to a jury,
with facts, passion, and determination, you might cut
your waiting time in half.

Tell them what you want,

and how you want it,

and make 'em do it for you,

just that way.

Let them know that the faster and more efficiently they do it, the sooner it will be over. Then you will go away satisfied, and they can go to lunch.

PRAISING MR. EHRENBERG

A great customer will praise a great employee. It is more thrilling to discover a "live" human being serving you than to have to fight against vegetables. Tipping is automatic in America, and usually has nothing to do with service. I once hoped that genuine intense praise would actually do the service provider some good. I was wrong. This involved the Fairmont Hotel in San Francisco, which is ironic because I think it is one of the most overrated in the world. It is famous for having been the setting for the television series *Hotel*, and you'll find groupies screaming for rock stars in every lobby. Somehow I ended up in this hotel, and after a week of mediocre service, I finally checked out. When I got to the airport for my next flight, I realized that I had left my airplane ticket, worth $1,200, sitting on the table in my room. I called the hotel immediately and, after some shuttling around on the phone, learned that the maid had thrown the ticket in the trash. That should have been the end of this story, but it isn't. An assistant manager at the hotel, Chris

Ehrenberg, took off his jacket, grabbed a couple of house-keeping workers, and climbed into the hotel's trash compactor looking for my ticket. He found it, and it was returned to me.

This was a deed so daring and so entirely out of sync with the rest of my experience that I wrote a letter to the owner praising Mr. Ehrenberg. I suggested the owner do the same, and requested an answer because I cared about the consequences.

Here is the owner's response:

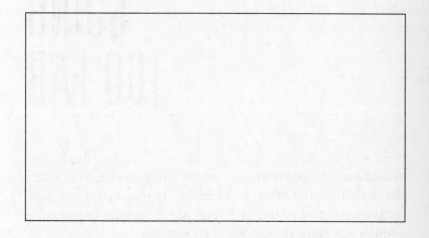

No response. The patient is dead. Nothing. *Niente*. *Nichts* Zero. Null. Void. *Rien*. Zilch. *Nada* word.

The owner does exist. Tributes to him in the form of photos of himself with "celebrities" crammed every page of the in-room reading material. But he was obviously too busy hosting Imelda Marcos in a complimentary suite to bother about the lowly clerks who actually deal with the sad and ordinary human beings who pay for their rooms.

I want to say to him, "Dear Owner, GO PRAISE YOUR EMPLOYEES if you want them to go down into the garbage to dig out a customer's valuables. If you don't, one of these days, Owner, they may take your valuables and put them into an incinerator."

I have never been back to the Fairmont, and I hope Mr. Ehrenberg is working his magic somewhere else, where it is better appreciated.

GOING TOO FAR

Sometimes you have to go "too far" to get what you want. But when customers are driven to it, that is exactly how far they go, and sometimes it spoils the whole experience even when they do get what they want.

Mary Alice Orito was wardrobe designer for the television serial *Search for Tomorrow*, and she regularly borrowed clothes to dress the cast, in return for program credits, from most any store in Manhattan—except one. This store was unique and important, so Mary Alice wanted to borrow clothes from it enough to push the matter. She had left twenty-seven phone messages with the store's owner, a famous ex–handbag buyer who ran her own show. Finally, Mary Alice sent her $275 worth of long-stemmed roses and a note. The note read, "Dear Madame: You do not answer my phone calls. I am sending you these roses in the hope they will be somehow

more persuasive. If, however, you do not answer this
message, I may have to send you an agitated skunk!"

Not a funny story, but the woman returned her call.

At Carnegie Hall I watched a "customer" going nuts
during a concert because the man in front of him was
making rattling noises as he slowly and constantly un-
wrapped caramels. He reached over the man's shoulder,
snatched the bag out of his hands, and handed it back
to him later, at intermission.

But best of all is the story (probably apocryphal,
whatever that means) about a mammoth passenger en-
throned in First Class on British Airways who was being
annoyed almost to death by a wild six-year-old girl who
ran up and down the aisle making noise continuously.
Her mother ignored her, which is something the parents
of children they can't control often do, and finally, with
the utmost exasperation, this giant Englishman turned to
the mother and said, "Madame, if you do not stop your
little girl from running up and down the aisles and making
this commotion, I am going to —— her!"

In its most dangerous form, customer activism is vigilante justice, and while it isn't right, the people who do
it often think that what is happening to them is grievously
abusive, and they feel they simply have to do something
about it.

For thirty years I could not get better seats at the
Metropolitan Opera, even though I was a continuous sub-
scriber all that time. Each year I sent a request for better
seats with my renewal and my money, and each year
they said, "Sorry. No better seats available at this time."

I finally wrote to the manager of the subscription
department, a tower of power who only ever said, "No."
I said, "I am almost deaf. For thirty years I have requested better seats to no avail, and I have always felt
that one of the best parts of going to the opera is being
able to hear it. Please help spare me the humiliation of

having to cancel my subscription because of my extreme age."

My seats were changed to fifth row, center. I am not proud of what I did to get there. I went too far. But I have enjoyed every moment of every performance since that time.

VICTIMS OF EDUCATION

Students are often victims when they go to school. You don't need to wait to go to college to encounter lousy teaching, but that's when most people first become customers with the power of choice. There are thirty or forty million students in this country today, and almost none of them realizes that he or she is a *customer*. It costs about $45,000 to get a college education these days. It's one of the biggest investments we ever make in "service," but most students take whatever they are handed, investigating nothing, enduring it all, and paying dearly for it.

From the beginning, students are conditioned to act grateful. "I was just so lucky to get accepted by Stanford," they snivel, saying good-bye to high school. None of this answers the question of whether students get what they pay for, once they enter ivy-choked halls. Do they spend four years being intimidated by tradition, or do they learn to think? The University of Michigan may have fifty teachers all teaching the same English course. Which ones are the best? Which one will the student get? Ninety percent of the time, the answer is, "the one I am assigned."

The problem with many teachers is that they resent teaching. They see it as a necessary evil that supports their writing habit. Or they just stick it out until they get tenure, which means they can practically never be fired, and then the quality of their teaching matters even less. Many teachers are just failed scientists or writers, secretly wishing their unpublished works would get published so they could get out of the classroom and appear on television talk shows.

A student has the right to interview the person teaching the course. If the teacher refuses the interview, why would you want anything more of that teacher? Find someone who doesn't flinch when you introduce yourself as a customer in search of great service. Ask questions:

"Why should I take this course?"

"Why should I take this course from you?"

"What are you like as a teacher?"

"What will I learn here?"

"What do I have to do to earn an A?"

Find out if the teacher plans to actually teach, or just reread the notes she or he has been rereading for the last eighteen years.

When you find a teacher who inspires you, take every course that teacher teaches; the quality of what will happen to your brain is far more important than the material you put into it. The hope is that a great teacher will teach you to think and grow, rather than memorize the geological eras in chronological order, or rules of Spanish grammar.

The difference in education is not as much the school you go to as it is the teachers you encounter there. There are lousy teachers at Harvard and excellent teachers at the University of Arizona, which I know is mostly a mammoth education factory. I know this about the University of Arizona because I went there.

My great teachers didn't happen to me. I learned to find them.

In my first year I didn't shop for teachers. I took whatever I got. I got teachers who couldn't even make their voices carry, much less teach, and teachers I couldn't understand, and teachers who never knew me by name. At the end of one expensive year, I had learned only one thing: My education, like every other service I would ever buy, was going to be my own responsibility.

SHOPPING FOR DOCTORS

Dr. Henry Baylis, a pioneering ophthalmologist, tells this story about himself:

SHOPPING FOR DOCTORS

I dreamed that I died. I showed up at the registration desk in front of Heaven. I went to the front of the line, and said, "I'm Dr. Baylis. My time is kind of valuable. I'd like to get into Heaven right away."

The attendant said, "Sorry, get back in line just like everybody else."

So I went to the back of the line. Suddenly this guy comes by carrying a black bag and wearing a stethoscope. He goes to the head of the line and the attendant thumbs him right on inside.

So I went back up to the head of the line again and said, "Lookit. You just waved that guy right on in, but you told me that doctors have to wait in line like everyone else."

The attendant told me, "That was no doctor. That was God. He's just acting like he's a doctor."

Are you intimidated by doctors?

Do you really think your doctor has the healing power of God?

Does that mean you must act "patient," instead of like a customer?

Doctors need to reread the Hippocratic oath. It's all about customer service. It says that doctors are bound to serve their patients. Most doctors forget this the first day after graduation.

Patients should read it to their doctors. They are customers, paying for service, but they seem to forget that truth when "the doctor" arrives (late) on the scene. There are 225 million customers in America who are doctors' patients, and patient is the last thing they should be.

If I were motivating a roomful of physicians, I would tell them, "Even though you are doctors, you may have forgotten that you are in the service business. I don't expect anyone in this room to believe that, but if I were talking to a roomful of patients, they would by now be enthusiastically pounding on the desks."

Isn't it most ironic that for the privilege of paying a doctor $200 for a twelve-minute audience, you, the customer, must show up on time so you can wait three hours, never complain—and don't ask to use the phone or the bathroom—while he finishes saving other lives? If you are prepared to shop for a doctor, you should expect to "interview" a few candidates.

Best-selling doctor-author Bernie Siegel once told medical students at Columbia University that if he were designing their curriculum, he would have them have their own blood drawn, have their chests X-rayed, and then be told, "We're concerned. We'd like to put you in the hospital for observation." Siegel said that he'd let the students lie there for three days before telling them it was all just a mix-up and they were really fine. Siegel told the students, "You'd never forget what it's like to be a patient."

Dr. Robert Liebert, a New York psychoanalyst, once asked me who my family doctor was. At the time, it was someone who lived in my apartment building. Dr. Liebert persisted. "Well, what's he like?" And I said, "I don't know. He's just a nice old fart who gives me my flu shots. Every time I see him he's working a crossword puzzle." I realized that was a silly way to pick a doctor. I needed to start shopping.

Dr. Liebert said, "Your doctor should be smart enough to earn your trust, new enough to have less than thirty thousand patients, and young enough so that he will probably die after you. And he should have both confidence and spirit."

"Try this man," Dr. Liebert continued. "If you don't like him, try another. But do it." So I called Dr. I. M. Best. He gave me a general physical, which cost $250.

This kind of research is expensive, but it is also a great test of a doctor. How much does he explain? How do you like him? How do you think he likes you? Or did he say, "You're fine. That will be $250."

You must search for a doctor as seriously as you search for a lifetime companion. That's what the two of you are going to be for each other. You need complete confidence in your doctor because he is treating your whole self, not just, say, your stomach. Your stomach is certainly part of you and it may have an ulcer, but if your doctor sees you as an *ulcer*, he is not treating *you*. He must make you his partner in your treatment. You should be consulted as surely as he is. You must understand all your options, and participate in deciding and planning your treatment. The final decisions are always your responsibility, so you'd better know full well

---

What you want,

and how you want it,

so that when you need it,

you'll get it just that way.

You don't need to know details of the inner soul of the dermatologist who burns one wart off your finger. And if your doctor has to tell you that if you don't have your appendix out in the next two hours, you'll be dead, your own opinion is not necessary. But it isn't usually as clear as that. It needs to be a working partnership as thorough and committed as any other you have.

Interview your doctors. Ask them to explain their views, their responsibilities, and their methods. Ask everything you want to know. How do they treat pain? Will they accept your "living will"? Have they just closed on a Palm Beach condo, and will they be abandoning you to the person who buys their practice six weeks from today? There are no guarantees about medical treatment. But if they don't want to talk about it, maybe something is wrong.

I would ask a doctor, "Tell me a couple of examples of how patients left you." If the doctor does not wish to explain some of the circumstances under which his patients quit, or why he may be late for your appointments, then you have your answer. No answer *is* an answer. You are establishing the terms of your relationship, and what you learn about this person could save your life.

When I went to Dr. Best, he *was* much younger than I was, I *was* among his first thirty thousand patients, and he *did* remember my name. When my friend Sam had cancer, he needed a great doctor. I recommended Dr. Best. But by now Dr. Best was successful, busy, and frequently late. He didn't answer calls, and he would often not call back.

Sam, as the customer, said, "I don't think this is the right doctor." And, indeed, Dr. Best was not being the right doctor. I said, "Inasmuch as he's a lot better than everybody else you know"—a dangerous thing to say because it's like saying he's not too bad—"why don't you go and talk to him about your relationship? Motivate him. What is the worst that can happen? Dr. Best can say, 'My other patients don't criticize me.' Fine. It's very important that you don't go to him if he doesn't like your terms."

Sam then had a conference with Dr. Best. He told him everything he liked about him, told him everything he didn't like about him, and, since this was *his* money, asked him how did that strike him? After that, Dr. Best did not change his personality, but he did pay attention.

SHOPPING FOR DOCTORS

That was a big change. He did show up on time. He did call back. He understood what the customer wanted. Obviously, if somebody in the next room is having a brain seizure, nobody is going to whimper about having to wait for an X ray. But it is nonetheless your responsibility to tell the doctor

---

> What you want,
>
> and how you want it,
>
> and make 'em treat you,
>
> just that way.

Suppose you have a doctor who always makes you wait. It used to be people didn't go to a doctor because they couldn't afford the cost. Today people don't go to the doctor because they can't afford the time. What do you do? You go to the doctor and you say, "Dr. Fox, I am the customer and I hate waiting. You always make me wait. How can we solve this? I can be your first patient of the day. I will get up at four o'clock in the morning. I will come here before you do and stand outside the door. I will calculate the average amount of time you make me wait and I will always come that many minutes late to my appointment, or I will charge you for my waiting time. Doctor, help me. What should I do?"

If that doesn't work, tell the doctor that you are going to change doctors, and ask him how much he values your business. He may tell you that he has a waiting list a mile long. Then you must decide if it's important enough to change doctors. To the next doctor you interview, you should say, "I'm really glad you graduated from Yale Medical School. But what I really want to know is, how punctual are you?"

If, on the other hand, Dr. Fox says, "I'm the best doctor in the world and you should be here. I'll try not to be late, but I'm certainly not promising you that you are never going to sit in my waiting room—for which I have ordered many lavish magazines." You must then ask yourself, Is it that bad? Could it be worse? Dr. Fox might say, "You're waiting only forty-five minutes. You could be waiting three hours. Wait till you meet Dr. Weasel. He *really* keeps people waiting." Or, "Why don't you move to Wyoming and get a doctor who never keeps you waiting because he has no patients and no CAT scanner?"

Service is really worth fighting for, but never more so than in a hospital where you are still a customer and you are helpless and scared. Sometimes you are fighting for your life. But there are agents even in a hospital. Many people don't know that in every hospital there is a nursing supervisor whom you can talk to if you aren't happy with the care you are getting.

One day when I was visiting Sam, who was having a very tough time in the hospital, a nurse that neither of us had ever seen before came through the door with a frown on her face and barked, "Sit up! You're supposed to sit up! You're supposed to get your exercise!" Sam was very weak and said, "I don't know if I can," to which she replied, "I'm *supposed* to get you to sit up. So the sooner you do it the better."

At that point I became angry and I said, "Would you like to introduce yourself?" She whipped around and looked at me and said, "What for?" I said, "My name is Peter Glen and this is your customer. What is your name?"

She threw a fit. I don't think she had ever been challenged before. I didn't like her attitude, and Sam was in no condition to complain so I said, "Wait a minute. Let's go see the head nurse."

We needed a different nurse, one who cared. I didn't want to distress Sam further, and it was immediately clear that she was miserable and probably should never have been a nurse in the first place.

It took me a while to find the head nurse and to work past all the other nurses who didn't want me to make a fuss. But I found her anyway.

Dragging the offending nurse in with me, I entered the head nurse's office and said, "This nurse is not compatible with this patient. We need a different nurse." Silence. "I know that you allocate bodies by computer," I continued. "I'm sure you can make a change." More silence.

So I made a short speech about nursing as a profession and how humanity-inspired it could be and what's-her-name did not seem to be inspired by anything except what time she gets off work, and concluded by stating that she would not be serving Sam.

At last, the supervisor spoke: "How did you get into my office?"

I responded, "By walking past legions of your startled minions, and then by walking through your door." We got a new nurse!

Of course, no one can make hospital staff care if they don't want to. Sam tallied forty-five different employees who served him one way or another during a two-week stay. They did everything from cleaning the halls to abdominal surgery. He came up with a total of four out of all these people who he thought really cared. Two were nurses who appeared to love nursing. The others were an oncologist and the surgeon. No one else showed that they cared. That doesn't mean they were negative. They just did their jobs with the same overworked "It sucks!" attitude of the counter girl at the Dunkin' Donuts.

Another day an unfamiliar nurse wheeled in an EKG machine. I happened to be there as she entered the room.

"What's that?" I asked.

"It's Mr. Dunn's EKG," she snapped.

"Who's the doctor?" I asked, as I couldn't understand why Sam needed an EKG. His heart was fine.

"It's Dr. Sanchez," she said.

"We've never heard of any Dr. Sanchez," I said. "Are you sure?"

"Well, it says right here that this patient is supposed to have an EKG, so I'm here to give it to him," she said in a loud, irritated tone of voice calculated to shut me up.

But we sent her away until we could get some confirmation. In fact, Dr. Sanchez was not Sam's doctor, and this woman was trying to give him another patient's EKG. It was a mistake! We wondered what might have happened if Dr. Sanchez's patient had died because an early warning of a heart attack wasn't detected? What if it had been surgery? Nurses have been known to give the wrong shots to the wrong patients and hospitals have been known to maim and kill people by mistake. Then they shrug and claim, "I'm only human," which is fine, except their patient now no longer is.

If you get out of a hospital alive, you then have to cope with a multipage bill that is written in abbreviations, codes, and acronyms so you can't tell how badly you are being hosed. When Sam checked out of the hospital there was a charge on his bill for $125 for the EKG he wasn't supposed to have and didn't get. Read your hospital bills. They are often wrong. The People's Medical Society of Emmaus, Pennsylvania, a nonprofit patient advocacy group, claims an audit of hospital bills found 98 percent of them are inaccurate, 75 percent of the time in the hospital's favor.

Customers need to fight for health care. You *can* say "No." Most patients think they have some sort of obligation to please the doctors and the nurses. It is the other way around. You have the right to see your own medical records, although in some states it is easier to get your FBI file. The anxiety of dealing with the unknown is far worse than the truth, no matter how tragic it may be.

Wouldn't it astonish you if you ever got a thank you note from your physician? Well, such a thing has actually been known to happen. Dr. Spenser Phillips Thornton of Nashville thanks his patients in a special, personal way. Dr. Thornton is one of our leading practitioners of radial keratotomy, the Russian-pioneered laser procedure which corrects defects of vision, frequently eliminating the need for eyeglasses, by literally reshaping the eye lenses. But almost equally amazing is the flowering azalea that Dr. Thornton sends each patient. It is one of the first things his customers see after the operation.

Another ophthalmologist, Dr. Corboy of Honolulu, sends a limousine to collect the customer and whoever is accompanying them, and transports them in comfort and luxury to and from the operation. Imagine leaving a hospital with bandaged eyes and trying to find a taxi! This stunning and thoughtful pleasure (a slight expense in a $3,000 to $6,000 operation) adds a memorable touch of humanity to what otherwise is, at best, an experience of both hope and anxiety to every customer.

Why is this so odd and unusual? If ophthalmologists were made to search for a taxi just one time after an operation on their eyes, the list of plants to be delivered and limos waiting outside would be multiplied within the twinkling of an eye.

You need to learn to become a strong shopper for

every service you seek. It's hard to imagine telling an architect what you want and expecting him or her to listen, but you must do it. It's your house and you are going to have to live in it. You need to shop for accountants and lawyers and insurance agents just as urgently as you shop for doctors, if you care about the service you're going to get. All of these providers can be intimidating, and probably will be surprised at your initial interrogation. But a gentle "C" sign shows that you are the customer and it is your money that pays their bills, and will usually serve to bring out the best in them.

Too many students are intimidated by their teachers. Too many honest people are easily upset by the folks at Internal Revenue. One of the tragedies of many managers is that they are intimidated by their own employees. This intimidation is not right, and it hampers all of them from getting what they're paying for!

Each of these people want your money, and all of them are there to serve you.

You are the customer! Shop! Interview! Demand!

Tell them what you want,

and how you want it,

and make 'em give it to you,

just that way.

THE ULTIMATE CUSTOMER SERVICE

As a customer, the toughest fight you ever have may be for your right to die.

Most people act as though they think that they will never die.

Thinking about death is dreaded so much that only one third of the adults in America leave a will when they die or leave instructions on medical care. And only about 15 percent of adults in America have living wills.

Everyone plans for buying a car, and perhaps college, and a wedding or two, and a house and children. And most are motivated to get insurance and to use their seat belts and to get smoke detectors. But they don't make out a will, which is easy and cheap to do. Even fewer have living wills, because they cannot visualize themselves as a prisoner of a life without dignity, with no recovery possible. So they go on thinking they'll just deal with it *if* it happens.

This is irresponsible. Death sometimes happens. And when it does the irresponsible person leaves behind for those most loved the instant burden of confusion, turmoil, cost, and grief.

A living will is not a legal document, because euthanasia is illegal in America. Most living wills urge an end to life-support treatment, but they can also be written to specify the conditions of prolonged treatment. Writing a living will is a responsible act.

When hope is gone, and death is near, and life is unacceptable, a person may want the *right* to die. The patient becomes a "customer." The customer is saying, "Please help me!" And someone will need to provide that service.

The right to die is unresolved in America, and it is controversial everywhere. But it is possible to observe this service in the Netherlands, where every year doctors perform euthanasia on two thousand to six thousand people. The Dutch call it "the gentle death."

Henk Rigter, the executive health director of the Health Council of the Netherlands, says,

> five years ago, every established medical organization condemned the Netherlands for our stand on euthanasia—our Nazi policies, they called them. Today Britain, Canada, the United States, and others are talking seriously about whether the need for it exists in their own medical systems. Now articles appear, and afterwards we receive phone calls asking how to get one-way tickets to the Netherlands.

In the Netherlands, the penalty for euthanasia is twelve years in prison, but if doctors follow certain guidelines they will not be charged.

> There must be an explicit and repeated request by the patient to be killed. The physical or mental pain must be severe and without hope of relief. The patient's decision must be of free will and enduring. All other options must either be exhausted or refused by the patient. The doctor must consult another physician and must record for the local prosecutor all events leading up to the final hour.

So even in the Netherlands, the patient is entirely responsible for initiating this service.

That is a lot of "C" signs for a customer to make to a service provider.

For a customer, this is even harder in America. There is conflict here, and a mighty, mixed bureaucracy, including the government, family and friends, insurance companies, the law, doctors and hospitals, and, often, ethics committees (80% of Americans die in institutions). All of these have strong and often opposed opinions.

So, even here the customer must be especially strong. The customer is a lonely individual in this ultimate, personal situation.

The best customers will be the ones who, here as elsewhere, take responsibility for their lives. They come to this transaction wearing all the costumes of "the customer" that they have worn before. They may not even know what they need exactly in the way of service. But they know what they want: they want peace.

It is hard for providers, too. But even now, these "gentle deaths" already take place in America.

The best providers will be those who have clear and confident minds. They have prepared themselves and now are ready to go on to serve customers, to understand what they want, to provide the service, and to say "goodbye."

The ultimate service this customer wants is peace. And the service that brings it can be called love.

The highest form of service is Love.

BRAIN SURGERY AT HOME

The service revolution is already under way at home. Customers and providers are discovering that "home" is a profitable place for service. People live and work there and are comfortable and safe there more and more. In 1989 over twelve *billion* catalogs were mailed to homes in America.

My friend Helen Brower has mastered the art of getting service at home. "Home" is where she lives and works and is most comfortable. Helen sees "room service" as a high form of human existence. She does not mean "room service" in hotels; she means getting the best possible service *in the room*. Service that comes to her. She hasn't been in a retail store in years, but is successful and well-dressed. She has mastered catalog shopping, paying bills and banking by mail, and ordering postage stamps and pizza by telephone. She has been a travel agent and is now a travel writer, so her list of agents is comprehensive. One of her most favorite expressions is "Hand me the yellow pages."

Helen is not lazy. She is smart. She gets good service, but avoids most "customer service." And she will leave home enthusiastically whenever it is worth it. A Turner exhibition at the Metropolitan Museum of Art is worth it. Lunch at Le Cirque is worth it. A vacation in the Seychelles is worth it (although a lot of trouble to get to).

Helen knows that there is no substitute for seeing the Parthenon in person, but if you decide to skip it, you will avoid a lot of crowds and irritable babies, air pollution, garbage, travel delays, and aching feet. And you will not have the temporary illnesses that are part of any three-day trek through the mosquitoes of Cozumel.

You will experience less by staying home, but you may enjoy it more.

Helen knows that doctors and lawyers and English professors do not usually make house calls. But even when she goes out to attend classes, she spares herself a depressing stop at the dry cleaners. She knows she has choices.

We all have choices. We can either stand in line at the post office or call Federal Express. Federal Express costs more, but you can count on them. And your time at home is worth something.

Don't misunderstand; Helen is a good customer. She knows

What she wants,

and how she wants it,

and she usually gets it,

just that way.

This year Helen solved the Christmas tree problem. Shouldn't it be a joy to get a Christmas tree? It should be a shining rite that binds the family together. And it is always a customer service experience.

"Dashing through the snow/ in a one horse open sleigh/

o'er the fields we go/ laughing all the way"—except that's not the way it usually happens. Most of us do not live in pristine northern climates, nor do we drive one-horse sleighs in the whirl of the winter winds to find our tree.

If you live in New York City, you can either pay an outrageous price for a spindly tree of unknown dryness from your nearby Korean grocer, or you can embark on a freezing excursion through the battered streets and be guaranteed a slushy adventure. When you finally pick a tree, you must prepare to find a taxi to take you and your new adoption back to your apartment. Fifteen cabs will pass you by because you want this tree and they don't. When you finally get home, you dump the tree in a bucket because you cannot find a saw, and you fix yourself a drink. If this year's Christmas tree is going to be a radiant adventure, it has not started yet. *"It's Christmas time in the city!"*

But if you don't live in the city, you drive through winter traffic to the mall, where you park at the farthest end of the parking lot, doomed to trudge through filthy gray and drifted snow and thirty thousand cars until you finally reach your goal: a roped-off part of the parking lot filled with dying trees illuminated by three naked bulbs.

The people selling these trees are colder and warier than you are. They are not enjoying themselves. And you are going to ask them to untie more than one tree so you can see what you're buying and what it's going to look like at home.

Thirty-five million people buy a real tree every year. Almost that many buy an artificial tree. It is no longer true that "only God can make a tree." You now can have a polyvinyl chloride substitute—"a thermoplastic resin . . . that is characterized by chemical inertness, resistance to weathering, electrical resistivity, and rigidity." If the branches look like bottle and toilet-bowl brushes, that's because they are made by the same machinery. If you buy one, you can avoid the freezing tree lots, arguing with your spouse, and vacuuming up those pesky falling needles. Your tree will not have gaps or sap or unsightly spaces between the branches. And you can just forget that for centuries people have brought the real thing indoors as an affirmation of life in the dead of winter.

So what's a customer to do?

A customer could do what Helen did as she sat at home reading the Smith and Hawken catalog, when suddenly she saw the following copy:

FRASER FIR TREE

From the Blue Ridge Mountains of North Carolina, the Fraser Fir has long been considered the very best Christmas tree because of its fragrance, excellent needle retention and lush foliage. Each tree is cut to order and delivered with haste and care. We guarantee that you will be satisfied. The trees are shipped in a handsome box with a greeting card should you request it for gift orders. And to brighten the tree, we've located miniature lights that are battery-powered. Each 20-light, ten-foot set liberates you from the need of a nearby outlet or extension cord.

And then you read this customer letter:

I feel obligated to write and express my appreciation for such a truly beautiful tree. It was all that you claimed and gave us many hours of pleasure. This mail order tree was a first for me. I was somewhat apprehensive until its arrival. You and your sources are to be complimented. It was still so fresh when we took it down yesterday that I felt guilty. I'm anxiously looking forward to next Christmas!

So you order it. You have just purchased a perfectly shaped, fresh and fragrant Fraser fir tree, and it will be presented to you at your door, on time, in perfect condition, totally guaranteed, in a sturdy box with clear calligraphic instructions. And the trunk is already scored across the bottom so you don't have to find a saw and attack it, dripping sap onto your living room carpet.

It costs about $84, including shipping. This is about as much as you would otherwise spend driving or taxiing around in traffic, selecting, trying to visualize, deciding, buying, and transporting your tree yourself.

You won't see your tree until the day it arrives, but relax! An expert is choosing it for you, so enjoy getting ready for Christmas at home until your tree arrives and brings you *"tidings of comfort and joy"*!

Customers and providers should, like Helen, work to perfect the art of service at home. "Home" is where the customer lives and works more every day, and it is a great place to provide service. If every American family and every American provider improved the service experience, it would cause a small but thorough revolution.

Helen has used her ingenuity and rights as a customer to create more of what she wants: productive time. She buys service to create time to work comfortably and productively, writing, which is what she wants most to do. Helen is a *great* customer.

If she ever needs to have brain surgery, she is going to try to have it done at home in her living room!

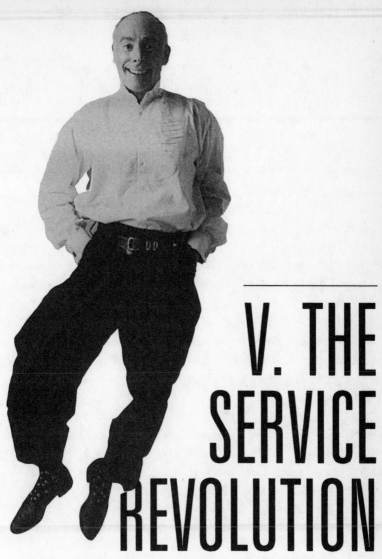

V. THE
SERVICE
REVOLUTION
BECOMING A BETTER SERVICE PROVIDER

To become a great service provider

> "Find out what they like,
>
> And how they like it,
>
> And let 'em have it,
>
> Just that way."

Suddenly it seems that every company in America has undergone a religious conversion to customer service. The hordes of the new faithful are scribbling about service in annual reports and sermonizing in interviews, and shouting from podiums in sales meetings. They commission more manuals, print more slogans, watch more videos, hire more consultants, and in general dwell in the fervent ecstasy that often awaits transfiguration.

Some of the prophets being heard from sound pretty good:

- "Customers are first, employees second, shareholders third, and the community fourth"—that's the credo at H. B. Fuller, the century-old adhesives maker in St. Paul.

- "We learned to pay attention to the customer," says John Fleming, Cadillac's general director of marketing and product planning. Developing a comeback following falling sales drove home "a very tough lesson."

- "Knowing what's on the customer's mind is the most important thing we can do," says Du Pont's Chairman Richard E. Heckert.

Sam Walton runs the most successful company in retailing, Wal-Mart stores. He has also been called the richest man in America. Sam puts it this way:

OUR CUSTOMERS

There is only one boss, and whether a person shines shoes for a living or heads up the biggest corporation in the world, the boss remains the same. It's the customer! The customer is the person who pays everyone's salary and who decides whether a business is going to succeed or fail. In fact, the customer can fire everybody in the company from the chairman on down, and he can do it simply by spending his money somewhere else.

Literally everything we do, every concept perceived, every technology developed and associate employed, is directed with this one objective clearly in mind—pleasing the customer.

Sam M. Walton

Right now there is an epidemic of this wisdom. Executives everywhere congratulate themselves on the clarion sound of their own voices evangelizing service. It sounds just great.

But is it true? Is this real service? Mechanical service? Lip service? How long will it last? It is, as many providers are finding out, more easily scribbled and sermonized and shouted about, than done.

How do you become a great service provider? Managements spend years and fortunes trying to motivate their service people. Companies spend lifetimes thinking up ways to motivate employees. We give them goals and objectives and targets and philosophies and mission statements and incentives and encouragement and training and retraining, we send them to seminars and counseling and est, we live through complaints and strikes, we treat them nicely, pay them and hope they will love us.

We long for that rare occasion when they do what we tell them to do and for which they get paid. And there will be more books and tapes and videos and courses, but most experienced managers would finally agree that you must treat customers as if you were getting paid for your services—because you are.

It is wrong to expect initiative; rejoice if you ever find it, but don't count on it. Maybe those five or six self-motivated people that you might meet in a lucky lifetime don't need your, or anybody else's, attention, but everybody else does need to be motivated—and not just once. It is a job that never ends; life seems to wear down people's enthusiasms, not with a bang, but with a whimper.

And you will have to tell them what to do every step of the way. You may think this is pessimistic and cynical, and gives employees very little credit for motivating themselves, but how many self-motivated people have you ever met? Six? Four?

BAD SERVICE BEGINS WITH "BODIES"

Good and bad service begin right at the beginning. Bad service starts with hiring. America is plastered with Help Wanted signs, but not one of them says what they want the "help" to do. And the jobs sound dull from the beginning. When Windows on the World wanted exceptional waiters, they ran an ad in *New York* magazine that went right to the heart of the matter; it said, "Waiters and Waitresses! If you have any interest in yourself, quit your job this afternoon and apply at 'Windows on the World.' " Hordes showed up immediately, with some anticipation.

> A lot of people have fancy things to say about customer service, including me. But it's just a day-in, day-out, ongoing, never-ending, unremitting, persevering, compassionate type of activity.
> —Leon Gorman, President, L. L. Bean

Consider the crisis at fast-food outlets. There isn't a hamburger joint anywhere in recent years that hasn't had a Now Hiring sign in its window. First of all, we're

BAD SERVICE BEGINS WITH "BODIES"

Americans, so we'd rather not work at all. Secondly, when most fast-food companies hire these people they are often so grateful to have what they actually refer to as "bodies"—a personnel term—that they expect "bodies," hire "bodies," educate "bodies," train "bodies," and then shove "bodies" out in front of customers.

You won't find an American company that doesn't claim to have a training program to inform and motivate new employees. Sometimes this program is two minutes long and consists of the rote recitation of a few rules such as "Do not steal or you'll be fired," "Do not commit a crime," and maybe, "If you are late, 1,740 times, you will be fired." Not one word about serving the customer. Nothing about discipline or creativity or fun or aspiration. It is well known, for instance, that security guards can be hired with no qualifications at all, and are often hired without even investigating whether they have a criminal record. You are likely to be guarded by someone who would know more about killing you than saving you. Ray Brunner, president of Conran's Habitat U.S., an English company, stopped paying $9.00 per hour for guards at the front of every store. He hired talented actors instead as courteous doormen—and guards.

The biggest problem in providing good service is that most employers never talk about it in the first place. Compare that with McDonald's Hamburger University or Disney's Casting Department. Or Stew Leonard being out in the parking lot with a retarded kid explaining to him how to stack up carts exactly the way they should be stacked. On your first day at Nordstrom in the shoe department, it would be explained to you that when a customer asks to try on a pair of shoes, you must bring out three pairs: the pair the customer requested, a second pair in the same style but a different color, and a pair of the hottest-selling shoe that week.

Good service is specific. It isn't, "Thou shalt provide good service and now we'll pause for music and meditation during which service will flood your soul."

Service means a thousand specific disciplined examples and then the company can say, "Now that you've got all that straight, let's tell you the history of Walt Disney and how he first drew Mickey Mouse." Service training from the very first discussion needs to be divided into regulations and discipline, and then *the joy of service*.

People that care are created. I don't think people are born longing to serve humanity. They are born needing to be cared for, and unless they are interrupted, they go on feeling the world should care for them forever.

The companies I know that provide good service put money and energy into sorting out the applicants who might be interested in becoming good service providers. British Airways, This End Up, Disney, and others think it is very important who you hire, not how many you hire. You can only train so much. It's better to pick the right people in the first place than to try to create a great employee out of a person who is just there to collect a paycheck.

Each company comes up with its own system, but if I were designing a sieve to catch the good ones, I would ask each potential employee a few specific questions about herself or himself. I would try to find out whether a person wants *this* job or if this job is just a second-rate version of what he or she really wants. I would ask applicants to describe how they feel about meeting the public. How do they feel about themselves? You can't make people happy, but you can hire happy people.

Libby Brown, executive vice president and the person in charge of customer service at This End Up, a chain of furniture stores, explains that in the interview process her personnel people ask a lot of theoretical questions: "What kind of person do you like to have wait on you?"

"How do you like to feel when you are a customer?" "What can you absolutely not tolerate as a customer?"

"An answer that would make us look twice at a candidate would be 'I can't stand it when a salesperson hangs over me and asks me a lot of questions.' A good answer would be, 'I like to go into a store where they are interested in what I need and me as a person but give me the space to make my decisions. When I need them they are there, but leave me alone when I want to be.'

"We're looking for balance," she says. "We prefer that they haven't worked in retail before, but if they have, we will ask them what was the most enjoyable part of the previous job, what was the most important part.

"We believe training begins with the hiring process. We have something called our 'shared values,' which is a list of ten things we believe very strongly in and is the basis for all of our decision making, whether you are a keypunch operator, a carpenter, a delivery driver, or on the floor. We show it to our people before we offer them a job because I want to look them in the eye and hear them say that they can live with that.

"The number one 'shared value' is to maximize sales, and the number two 'shared value' is happy customers. We ask if they can live with this every day under all circumstances, and we expect them to know it before we offer them a job."

When Libby presents new applicants with her list of shared values, and asks them to comment, she has the advantage that they could not have seen it before. Their answers tend to be spontaneous and therefore revealing. She is able to find out exactly how that person would fit into her organization. One of the great values of writing out a creed or a mission statement or a definition is that you can submit everyone to it. It is a statement of your standards. It can help you find out if applicants consider their job to be a humiliation or just a step on the way to something else, or whether it is something they really want to do. Are they going to be totally dissatisfied? Are they just needing to fill time?

The applicant can test the values of the prospective employer, too. There is a story about a young man who was interviewed for a job by Barney Pressman, the head of Barney's menswear store in New York. The young man, undoubtedly nervous, said, "Mr. Pressman, do you mind if I smoke?" The original "Barney" said, "No, but wait just a moment." He then opened his desk drawer, took out a surgical mask and put it on, and said to the applicant, "Okay, go ahead!"

When it was a flop, British Airways used to hire on the basis of technical competence, and it encouraged employees to focus on pleasing the bureaucracy of the organization instead of its customers. The new, privatized British Airways screens first for people who enjoy working with customers. The technical stuff comes later.

"You have to get people who enjoy treating people as individuals and who are prepared to accept responsibility for delivering what the customer wants," says British Airways' Michael Bruce.

"The problem is being clear about what it is you want more than deciding how you get it. One of the things we've done is train our best cabin crew and set them to the task of selecting new staffers. We gave them fairly rigorous specifications for what we wanted and prescribed the procedures by which they did it. These crew members were people who were proven good performers in the area of customer service. Given that people will tend to choose others in their own image and likeness, we found they picked other people who are also good with customers.

"The most *important* thing we do, however, is to listen to what the customer is saying. If our people don't understand what is motivating the customer, they won't be successful in handling them. We share the research we do on passengers with our employees, so they can learn how passengers react under stress, how they behave. Because of their stress, passengers blow things out of proportion and sometimes behave completely disgracefully. But they are still our customers. And how effectively we handle their problems while they are under stress very often determines whether they will remain our customers. Our understanding of things from the *customer's* point of view is critical."

Donald Hess, president of Parisian stores, says, "We look for people who smile when we are interviewing them, who are warm, who seem to have an understanding of how to deal with customers and how they would like to be treated. For years I would say to people, 'Just go out and treat customers the way you would like to be treated.' Then I realized that a lot of them had never been treated well in a store. So I wasn't making an impression on them.

"Now we teach, we try to set examples. Then we have our management lead by example. They deal with customers and rectify problems. A new sales associate, even though we tell them over and over again to do what's right, is going to be very hesitant. They are going to call a manager in to help them. Then when they see the manager deal with the customer, they learn what's expected."

The same is true at Stew Leonard's, where Stew Leonard, Jr., told me, "We hire on attitude, more than on the basis of any skills. Some people say you can't measure attitude, it's subjective. If he's really trying hard, we feel that same thing will happen on the floor. Some prospective employees come in wearing blue jeans with holes in them and big dangling earrings, chewing gum and all that. Basically that says the person doesn't care. If I put them on the floor, our customers are going to get the impression that we don't care."

At Stew Leonard's they train by example. "All our managers must look at themselves as the model," says Stew, Jr. "A lot of people sit there and say, 'Here's what we want you to do' but they don't do it themselves. We as owners believe in hard work. That means the people who work for us have to work hard too. We like people to come in early and stay late and work on weekends. That means we should be in there too. Not twenty-four hours a day but pop in at all different times. I come in some mornings at five o'clock and cook everyone breakfast."

So, most companies should fire the training director and burn the manuals. You have to train people to be themselves, the same as a psychoanalyst does. No formula exists that could possibly work for everyone. Nordstrom stores understand this. The company gives every new hire something they call an employee handbook but which is, in fact, a single card that reads as follows:

Welcome to Nordstrom. We're glad to have you with the company. Our number one goal is to provide outstanding customer service. Set both your personal and professional goals high. We have great confidence in your ability to achieve them. Nordstrom Rules: Rule #1: Use your good judgment in all situations. There will be no additional rules. Please feel free to ask your department manager, store manager or division manager any question at any time.

Employees at Matsuya, a small Japanese department store chain, receive two solid months of training before they encounter their first customer. The training manual talks about "co-existence and co-prosperity with the customer." Sales employees are reminded "to offer not only good merchandise but also one more value: your heart." The company's motto is "Respect for Humanity."

"SHE'S A BITCH AND WE LOVE HER"

There is an argument among all managers in this country about the best style of managing: discipline or creativity. If you were motivating Marines it would be simple. You wouldn't want creativity at all. You would give exact orders on making the corner of every bed perfectly. You'd inspect the bed. If it wasn't made perfectly, you'd assign latrine cleaning duty. The opposite is total creativity, where nobody tells anybody what to do. That is chaos. It is a fact that without discipline most people do nothing. People need to be told what to do, and how to do it. Then you have to go see if they did it, praise them if they did, and discipline them if they didn't.

Whenever you go by the front of a Hickory Farms store in a mall, there is always someone standing near the front handing out free samples. It's a rule. One day I tested it.

"What happens," I asked, "if you don't hand out samples?"

"We get into trouble," she said.

"What kind of trouble?" I asked.

"We get fired!" she said. "Is that trouble enough for ya? Here, try this cheese."

Great discipline means better service for the customer.

Disney is a creative organization, but it is first a

disciplined one. The company acquired a hotel in Orlando. Some of the hotel's staff members had worked there for a long time. It is a Disney rule that nobody may wear facial hair. Those staff members who didn't want to shave would have to go elsewhere. Some of the employees protested, but they either shaved their faces or they were fired. Disney also wants its employees to be funny, cute, ingenious, and entertaining. So, in effect, Disney is saying, "You can't wear a beard while you work for us, but you can be Snow White or one of the Seven Dwarfs." More importantly, they are saying, "We need you to say the basic script absolutely accurately on the African ride, and *then* we want you to add your own stuff."

When Disney opened a Disneyland in Japan, the discipline was easy. Its Japanese employees followed every instruction faster, sooner, cleaner, and neater than employees in Orlando had ever done. They could get them to do everything, with one exception: no one would improvise. Nobody was having fun, not even the customers. For the first time the Japanese are learning the value of creativity, and if they ever master it, they'll probably beat us in both discipline and creativity. Now Disneyland is opening in France, a country where no one has ever smiled. This ought to be a real challenge for the Mouse.

The mix of discipline and creativity is a question of balance and sequence. Michelangelo might have dreamed up his image of God creating man during a single glass of wine in the Piazza della Signoria. But he had to have the discipline to lie on his back for four years under wet plaster falling from the ceiling of The Sistine Chapel to get it done.

Associated Dry Goods is a company which no longer exists, but when it did it used to hold conferences for the top executives at expensive resorts. I asked thirty-seven of them how many had personally been in a Nordstrom store. Astoundingly, only seventeen had ever had the experience.

We immediately canceled afternoon golf, hired limousines so they would be happy and protected, and went to a nearby Nordstrom at South Coast Plaza. I had "guaranteed" them that there was no substitute for the in-store experience, and that in Nordstrom's shoe department every salesperson would bring out three different pairs of shoes for every customer, every time, no matter what the customer asked for.

We grumbled and limoed our way up to the store, and I preceded them into the shoe department. The CEOs were all standing behind me in their leisure clothing, watching the salespeople bringing out a lot of shoes. I stopped the department manager and asked him a question so that all behind me could hear his answer.

Well, I was wrong. When I asked the manager if it was true that the salespeople were required to bring out three different styles, for every customer, every time, he said, "No."

A rustle went through the CEOs behind me. I was possibly failing.

But the manager hadn't finished. "We make them bring out four pair. We figured if three pair was great, four pair was even better. We're very happy with the results."

Then the executives went back to the resort and played golf.

Discipline is something most companies hate to talk about and most managers hate to put into action. I once asked someone at Nordstrom, "What do you do if a salesperson *doesn't* bring out three pairs of shoes?" I wanted to hear it from his own lips, but I could not get an answer from him. He wouldn't say it.

The person I was asking said, "Well, they do."

"You're not answering my question," I said.

"But they just do," he said, "so I can't answer what happens if they don't."

What should management do when it catches an employee giving bad service? If I were a business owner and happened to overhear an employee telling a customer any version of "It's not my department," the first thing I would do is rush over to the customer and say, "It *is* *my* department. What can I do to make you happy?"

The first thing to do is save the customer, fast. The person who said "It's not my department," would stay right with me while we made the customer happy. Then I would make an example of the incident, rather than make an example of the specific employee, to impress the point on everyone else. I would consider calling a meeting of all my employees and say, "I just heard someone say 'It's not my department' to a customer." That's the discipline part.

Doug Tompkins, an owner of Esprit, the big clothing manufacturer, set up an exquisite carp pool in the employee's Japanese garden at Esprit's headquarters in San Francisco. There is also a microphone on the reception desk that broadcasts throughout the company—the offices, the loading docks, and so on. It's there for use in emergencies. One day Doug picked up the microphone and said, "I want everyone in the lobby, right now." The whole company stopped.

People came from various buildings and up and down stairs, and when he had hundreds of employees jammed into the front of the building, he held up a soggy cigarette butt and said, "I found this in the carp pond. I cannot bring myself to believe that some person in this room has thrown a cigarette into our Japanese garden. I don't care who it is, but I would like you all to know that if it ever happens again we will close the garden. Is that clear?"

The presence of a cigarette butt was an attack upon his *basic* philosophy about Esprit. More importantly, he sent a dramatic message about discipline to everyone working there, and I'm sure those people still talk about the day Doug Tompkins went insane over a cigarette butt. It is now part of the Esprit legend.

Another important aspect of the culture at Esprit was created the day Doug Tompkins first said: "It's the *last* ten percent that makes fifty percent of the difference."

At This End Up, the salespeople are encouraged to go out of their way to please customers. That is creativity. Although it isn't exactly a mainstay of the company's policies, employees know that they can bend the rules and even go outside of their budgets to deliver an end table that is left off the delivery truck.

Employees are encouraged to get on the phone and follow up with customers to find out how they like the furniture. That's creativity. They are encouraged to spend the money to send flowers to customers when it is appropriate. But first there is discipline.

"We decided several years ago that because we have a lot of young people and our turnover is high, we needed to simplify the before-the-sale customer service aspect," says Libby Brown. "So we tell them there are these three things they must do with every customer, no matter what, every time—or else they will be fired.

"The three musts are they must stand up and smile when a customer enters the store, they must get off the telephone as soon as possible"—one of my favorites— "and they must ask the customer two questions that have nothing to do with furniture."

Too few companies have rules. At The Footlocker everyone wears the black-and-white-striped uniform (or else), no one sits down in the store (or else), and no one smokes cigarettes or eats in front of customers (or else).

I think most businesses could live with those rules, and it would improve their sales. The Footlocker is a shining star performer in the frantic athletic shoe field.

Uniforms are another form of discipline. Uniforms are also a great way to tell who is a service provider and who is a customer. At Stew Leonard's, every cashier and many other workers at the store must wear a bright red shirt, provided to them by the company. If you wander into Stew Leonard's and want to find low-fat yogurt, it will take you about one second to find somebody who can tell you (nobody says "I don't know" and nobody says "Nine"), and you won't embarrass yourself and other shoppers by walking up and down the aisles asking, "Do you work here?"

The best companies of the future will balance discipline and creativity. That means the manager is going to have to be both a disciplinarian and a creative force. He must constantly compute which is which, what is the right proportion, what is the right sequence, what is right in an emergency, what is most important, what is most profitable.

One day I heard this discipline and creativity combination summed up once and for all by a seasoned San Fernando Valley saleslady who had been working at Judy's for a long time. Judy's was the first great "juniors" fashion store and Marcia Israel was its inventor and owner. I wandered into the store and saw a protégée standing by a blouse rack wearing substantial shoes and spectacles on a pearlized chain. I asked her, "What is Mrs. Israel like?" and she said it perfectly, *both* parts: "She's a bitch, and we love her."

Discipline first, creativity after. You need both.

"WE WON'T DANCE, DON'T ASK US"

Hundreds of companies have motivational meetings, and they spend hours and tears all year trying to figure out "what the theme should be this year." The theme is usually something inane like "Momentum" or "Challenge '93." I even attended a meeting where the theme was "It's a Whole New Ball Game," which was dramatized by the CEO having baseball bats passed out and demanding that the audience bang them on the floor while chanting, "It's a whole new ball game!"

We were trying to motivate six hundred managers at the Cloth World national sales meeting. Cloth World was inviting all its managers and their spouses, as well as divisional and regional and territorial managers, and every VP of everything. Cloth World was going to motivate the entire company in two days. Of course, it did not invite any of the twenty-four hundred employees who would be standing in the stores talking to customers while their managers were off getting motivated.

The event was being held in Amarillo, Texas. It was taking place at the (believe it or not) Pancho Villa Convention Center, a drafty concrete hangar, and the company planned to treat everybody right by throwing a huge party with a big band and unlimited snacks and drinks. The guests weren't expected to do anything. Management thought this would provide a lot of motivation. I disagreed.

The meeting had to be as powerful as possible, because God only knew how much of it would last until the big six hundred who attended got back home. I wanted to involve the management, although, believe me, it is difficult to get an "operating committee" to wear chef's hats and stand behind a buffet to serve breakfast to their people at 7:15 A.M.

So far we had nothing except an item which the company meeting planning committee was pleased to call its third or fourth "revised tentative agenda." This was a wimpy document assembled by far too many people and then sent forth for the approval of even more people.

It was time to tell them what to do to get everyone involved.

We asked all the regional managers to dance in a chorus line, wearing red-and-white-striped blazers and carrying boater hats and canes. They would entertain their people, offer a few rare glimpses of their humanity and creativity, and inspire by example.

We sent out invitations telling all the guests to wear red and white and black. This would look terrific and bind everyone together without limiting their individuality.

Everything backfired.

The regional managers instantly formed a bond, demonstrating the concept of a group, and raved. "We won't dance, don't ask us" was the way it was put. They were terrified of everything: of dancing badly, being laughable, looking foolish, and rocking the boat. I assured them they were right, they would be doing all those things, and asked that they just show up for rehearsal at two P.M. the day before the event.

The guests revolted, too. "You're not going to tell us what to wear. Who are you to tell us what to do?"

We had to write the invitation over again. We arranged the wording far more carefully, so as to be more motivational. We wrote, "If you wear red, white, and black, you will get in!"

At rehearsal the managers were taught some good, simple dance steps, and when they put on their blazers and hats and held their canes and looked into the mirrors in the dressing rooms, they saw themselves smiling.

The people showed up looking splendid in red, white, and black. And when the evening entertainment arrived, there was riotous excitement in the room as people watched their managers join the human race. That evening is still remembered not only as black and white and red night, but also as the night with such excitement that some of the guests even carried it back to the twenty-four hundred people in the stores—where it matters.

"HAVE YOU EVER TRIED PEACH SOUP?"

Breaking routine can sell a lot of peach soup, too. There is a restaurant in Denver where the approach of a waiter surprised everyone at our table and taught us a lot about service. Everything was normal—that is, invisible, routine, and dull—until the waiter approached the table. When he had our attention, he asked, "Have you ever tried peach soup?" The immediate answers varied from "Yuk!" to "Ugh!" to "No!" (Americans are perhaps their most articulate at the table.) But he had our attention and the meal was off to a roaring start. The soup was cold and tasted exactly like peach nectar. It was not revolutionary one way or the other. Peach soup is a best-selling item at that restaurant—because the people working there *sell* it. If they didn't, nobody would *ever* order it. But since they do make a point of selling it, the restaurant has become extremely famous as "that restaurant that sells peach soup."

I was so impressed I went around for years handing out little pleated paper cups of peach soup to audiences and telling them they had to overcome their fears and eat it before I would begin. People's reactions were extreme. They refused, argued, ate, and survived. Peach soup is a symbol of the unknown, and it terrifies people. It certainly breaks their routine. It is good for them. And it sells.

These are questions that I am constantly asked, and for which there are no definite answers:

Q. Can you measure the value of breaking routine?

A. Probably not.

Q. Does breaking routine make people act?

A. Sometimes, and sometimes not.

Q. If people do act, how long will it last?

A. It's as different as the number of people who experience it. And it is often as long as the management's persistence.

"HAVE YOU TRIED PEACH SOUP?"

Q. Is it worth it?

A. Read the following.

I led a group of General Foods executives out of White Plains, New York, and into the customer's world. We broke routine and made the most of it, talking all the way. We spent two days in New York City, experiencing what was new; each meal, hotel, and retail destination was chosen carefully.

We lived like customers, and then we discussed what we could do to serve our own customers better.

In New York, we stayed at Morgans Hotel. Morgans will not hire anyone to work there who was born in New York; Morgans maintains it gets better service from people coming from elsewhere. (Nordstrom has said it is reluctant to open a store in New York for the same reason.)

We had lunch at the Rainbow Room to inspect and understand the $26 million renovation. We toured new stores, playing the role of "customer," and attended the evening gala at Bloomingdale's "China" promotion—a major benefit for children with AIDS. Next morning we had breakfast at Bloomingdale's. The store personnel explained the making of the event. Julian Tomchin asked us, "Why don't you people make kiwi Jell-O? Kiwi is the newest fashion fruit, and you people still make lime. You'll sell more lime if you get more overall attention by making something new. Try cranberry. Or grapefruit."

For once, nobody said, "How do we fund it?" or "The product managers will never go for it" (the product managers were there!), or "We ought to run some focus groups." Instead, three days later, Brian Laragh, group vice president, led a group down into the kitchens at General Foods and tried it.

Meanwhile, someone, somewhere added vodka to Jell-O and now in bars across the country people are ordering

"Jell-O shots"—Jell-O for adults. Bloomingdale's already understood the idea of promotion perfectly. General Foods was just learning.

We toured California to study marketing to children, and San Antonio investigating the Hispanic market. Each of these trips ended with a session of resolutions whereby, after having traded ideas, we tried to convert the experience into a plan of action for each executive. These decisions had to be made before we went back to White Plains, where the halls are lined with corporate art and the silence throughout the award-winning architecture is like living underwater. Everyone now understands firsthand that the cereal boxes on the supermarket shelves in Texas have glue that is too thin and are shipped in cartons that are too flimsy; we have seen the cereal spill out of boxes that are crushed in the customer's grocery cart. The boxes in the board room are never crushed.

During another of these "wrap-ups" for Eaton's in Montreal, a furniture merchandise manager arrived for the final meeting in a state of considerable agitation. After three days of pounding the pavements looking at art and architecture and furniture, he now, as a final indignity, was being asked to show up with the rest of us in a SoHo loft that, though it was a brilliant and innovative design, still had to be reached by way of a really dirty freight elevator. The loft was a sequence of spaces and levels forming rooms without walls, and we were all about to sit on the floor, or on low dividers, or the piano bench, or a major wooden rocking horse.

Everyone sat down, somehow, in various degrees of comfort. One man, sixty years old and head of a $40 million furniture division, refused to sit anywhere, but stood in a corner by himself. It was everyone's turn to tell us their intentions. He spoke first. "When I saw this room," he said, "at first I thought we'd really gone too far. But finally I realized it was me who hasn't gone far enough. The thing that shocks me is that this room is my business, and I don't recognize a thing in it. My decision is to start all over again, to learn my business by pursuing it instead of letting it rule me, to try to watch for the comforting evils of routine, and to kill them before they get to me. I would like to sit down now and I cannot find a chair, so I will sit right here on the floor and I will probably enjoy it."

This man was upset by this experience. He was excited by his business. He was alive.

Life is not a matter of age, or time, or place, or success. It is a matter either of adventure or routine, and only when routine is banished are we really growing. T. S. Eliot wrote

> We shall not cease from exploration
> And the end of all our exploring
> Will be to arrive where we started
> And know the place for the first time.

Ideas are not enough. It is only action that matters. Brian Laragh, the sponsor of the General Foods excursions, first told me another T. S. Eliot quotation:

> Between the idea
> And the reality
> Between the motion
> And the act
> Falls the Shadow.

Providers of customer service—indeed, all people who want a more productive life—must watch for the shadow, kill it, and live in the blessed realm of action.

During these routine-shattering excursions, the participants are hit with plenty of ideas. But the only thing that matters is action. Nothing in the meeting matters as much as the last two hours, when everyone is asked to tell us, in two minutes or less, what they are going to *do* as the result of the past days' adventures. It is not enough to hear what hit them, what they liked or didn't like, or how they feel about any of it. The only thing that matters is what they are going to do.

Most of the participants find this very difficult. It is, after all, a *commitment*, not just an observation. The entire exercise aims toward these conclusions, for it is in the action that the company will, or will not, benefit from the exercise.

"My purpose in doing these trips was to use the various activities as a catalyst for individual action," Brian says. "The good and bad things that happen in a company are the result of individual effort. I think each of our people will learn to serve our customers better because they played their role for a couple of days. The basic thing I want our people to learn is that the world is much bigger than just our industry. You can learn particulars from other businesses that you can bring back and adapt for our own business."

Let's say you are not a group vice president of General Foods and you don't have the kind of money to spend flying people around the country and treating them to lavish parties and unforgettable meals. What can you do? If you are running a shoe store in a mall, I would say to your employees, "You've got forty-five minutes. Go up and down the mall and come back with three ideas on how to improve our customer service. You are not allowed to go into another shoe store and you are not allowed to go as an employee." I've done this with shop workers, and they all pour back into the room after forty-five minutes, and they *do* come back with ideas.

If I were running a small hotel in Honolulu, I would

take the heads of each of the departments—the banquet manager, the parking manager, the travel manager, the garden manager, the food planning manager, the housekeeping manager—and I would send them out and pay for them to stay at the best hotel in Hawaii, asking them to come back with a report on how we can improve service at our hotel. They would go as customers; nobody would know they were coming from another hotel. They would try to get a room like any ordinary customer. But I would warn them that they had better ask to see a choice of rooms, they should try to sit by the window in the restaurant, and they should experiment with every service in the guest directory.

They would have to come back with a report and suggestions to improve service in our hotel with the same staff, the same budget, in the same building, with no additional expenditures. They could not come back and say, "Our customers would be happier if our swimming pool were eighty feet longer."

I would make bank employees stand in line and try to open accounts.

If customers can get loans at my bank, I would have my employees apply for loans at five different banks. I would send them to savings banks as well as commercial banks and tell them to come back at three o'clock in the afternoon prepared to discuss their experiences. I would send the head teller to critique the tellers at the bank around the corner and come back with an idea for improving service. I would have someone open an account at another bank and maintain it so I could know how my competition provides service. Robert Winters, the chairman of Prudential Insurance Co., once opened an account at Fidelity Investments, a major competitor of his Prudential-Bache division. He wanted to see how Fidelity services its customer accounts.

The travel industry should study the hotel business

and vice versa. A doctor should show up with a medical complaint in the emergency room sometime. A real estate agent should pretend to be a home buyer and get another real estate agent to show him or her some houses.

What if every groggy professor was condemned to sit in a hard chair and listen to herself or himself for thirty hours a semester? Suppose the president of Eastern Airlines had been forced to eat what I was given to eat, or was welcomed aboard the "pig flight" to San Juan. This would start a revolution. Service *would* get better!

There is a lot of dutiful chitchat nowadays amongst service providers about "management by walking around" and "staying close to the customer." This saves the customer the trouble of using that token gesture, the open-door policy. I once passed by the open door of the office of the president of Eaton's of Canada department stores. A customer had made it all the way upstairs and through the open door and was at this point screaming at the president and enjoying herself immensely. By the time I moseyed by she was into her windup and was making it personal. "The trouble with you, Mr. Eaton," she shouted, "is that you've forgotten where the store *is*!"

She was right; he should have spent more time out on the floor. (Great expression, "on the floor." I once heard a salesperson pick up the phone in the cosmetics department at Filene's in Boston. She listened for a moment, and then said, "I'm sorry, she can't come to the phone right now. She's on the floor with Mr. Shapiro!")

Ray Brunner walks around his stores as president of Conran's Habitat U.S. He peers into managers' offices without warning and asks them, "What are you doing?" This is a very startling question that is sometimes not easy to answer. Ray never announces his visits to stores. Neither do customers.

When you visit "the floor" of your company, don't

announce it. Just go. Just put yourself into a normal car, try driving it yourself, try parking where customers park, then enter your store or your factory floor and think like a customer.

There are too many unself-confident executives who beef up their self-importance by frightening the inhabitants. There was a popular saying at Kaufmann's stores in Pittsburgh when David Farrell was president. People in the branch stores said, "When the brown Mercedes pulls into the parking lot, move your ass!"

I have seen meetings canceled and work stop almost completely when the grapevine shakes with the words, "A vice-president is coming!" One California factory was so intimidated by this kind of warning that they spent $100,000 to repaint the entire building inside and out for an impending visit by "the chairman," and then the chairman canceled his visit.

This is all backwards. The only alarm that matters is the one that sounds every time a customer pulls into the parking lot. The executive who rules by insecurity and intimidation will be shielded from reality and gain nothing from roaming the field except the faked-up adulation of the folks who have been warned that you are coming.

However, if you arrive unannounced, your managers may faint when they recognize you, your people will probably show themselves truly, and you can believe what you see and hear and act on it.

As far back as Shakespeare, smart executives have been playing the role of customer. Duke Vincentio in *Measure for Measure* announces he is leaving Vienna and appoints his deputy, Angelo, chief executive in his absence. Instead of leaving town, the Duke disguises himself as a Franciscan friar, and hangs out with the ordinary folk downtown. He gets an earful. He gets no lip service at all. He learns a lot about the city and the citizens and Angelo, unscreened by politics, and enough experience to resume being duke with genuine wisdom.

Today Hyatt Corporation executives close down their offices once a year and work as ordinary employees. Herbert Kelleher of Southwest Airlines rides his airplanes regularly, unannounced. David Sabey, new owner of Frederick and Nelson department stores in Seattle, introduced himself to his new employees via video teleconference—dressed as a store doorman. He said it emphasized the importance of customer contact.

Jimmy Martin was the only executive I ever met who had no office. He was a wonderful, eccentric man who ran the Myers' department store in Adelaide, Australia. He ran his store by standing in it, or by strolling around almost all day every day, sometimes sipping a beer. If he needed to make a phone call or hold a meeting, these took place on the floor in the store. If you wanted an appointment with Jimmy Martin, you walked with him while he walked through the store. Jimmy was listening to what you had to say, but he always kept watching his customers, every step of the way.

One day we went into the hardware department, and Jimmy suddenly saw customers but no salespeople. He solved it in an instant. At the top of his lungs, he yelled a single word—"HELP!"—just once. And it was enough. People appeared instantly from everywhere, salespeople, managers, maintenance men, and even some more customers joined the crowd around Jimmy in the hardware department.

There was not another word of explanation. They all knew Jimmy's voice and Jimmy's attitude. They knew what he wanted and how he wanted it, and they also knew they'd better give it to him, fast.

Try it sometime (whether you're a customer or a provider). Just go into a store and when you find that you can't get help, just stand there and scream the word as loud as you can. You will see people come running who haven't moved in years. You will be serviced, solicited, fawned upon. They will sing to you, if that's what you want, or anything else you want, as long as you don't *do that* again. You have embarrassed them by reminding them of their jobs, and they are also afraid someone else might hear and want the same thing.

Screaming HELP at the top of your lungs is a lot like making the "C" sign. It confronts the situation, calls a halt to routine, and starts alarms ringing everywhere. You get attention, suddenly and completely. You have just staged a small but specific revolution.

There is no substitute for playing the role of customer. And there is no way to do it, except to do it. Sam Walton manages to visit a hundred of his stores every year, in person. Stew Leonard and his family are planning for the extraordinary necessity of soon having to be in two stores at once. But many managers haven't been face to face with customers for years. They dwell in marble halls, isolated from life and reality, where they sit reading performance reports after the fact, and aging away upstairs in waves of nostalgia, far from the sweat, tears, and money of real life downstairs. If they were to hit the sales floor, they would cause the service revolution to take place from within, instead of making it the customer's responsibility. They would find *themselves* making the "C" sign, instead of getting it from customers. And they and their businesses would thrive.

NEVER SAY "I DON'T KNOW"

I once saw a customer staring at a television monitor over a meat display in a Loblaw grocery store in Canada. She was watching the president of the company, David Nichol, on videotape, giving a veal recipe. Twenty minutes later, the same woman was watching the same show, and I asked her what she was watching.

"I didn't get the oven temperature the first time," she said. "I have to watch it again."

The president of the company was selling this woman veal by giving her information on how to cook it. All good salespeople do this, and the presidents of more companies ought to understand how important and how persuasive information can be.

A friend of mine went into an Eddie Bauer sporting goods store one winter and found on sale a lightweight coat made with Gore-Tex. He'd wanted one for a long time, but the prices were beyond his budget. He wanted to know why it was on sale. He was afraid the coat was damaged or defective, which would make the price less attractive. He asked a clerk why the coat was on sale, and the clerk gave him a blank look like it was the stupidest question he'd ever heard.

"I don't know," he said.

"How can I find out?" my friend asked, trying to encourage the clerk to be his agent. The clerk hunted down the manager, who gave an answer that was not only logical but made my friend want to buy the coat that much more. The coat was on sale simply because it was out of season. The price would go back up in the spring. My friend had wanted an unlined coat in the first place, so he felt he got a great bargain.

The front of Macy's menswear store on Stockton Street in San Francisco stopped me cold. A Pirelli carpet rolled right out the store's front door across the sidewalk and down to the street. It was printed, "Tenere, Tenere, Tenere!" A huge sculpture of a male torso stood in front of the store, banners shouted "Tenere!" What may be the biggest single department store window in America continued the blast with more black and red and sculpture and banners and "Tenere!" and five male mannequins which were dressed in identical pairs of terrific black pants with many, many pleats and tight, ankle-clutching bottoms. There was a big fat frogged belt at every waistline. Terrific show. Terrific pants. But what *was* "Tenere"?

It was a new Paco Rabanne cologne for men, but I had to ask three people to find that out.

The staff was standing there spraying and wiping the counters and reconstructing their hair. The first staff had never heard of "Tenere"! I told her about the windows. "Oh," she said, "the staff come in from the back. Only customers come in off the street."

Was she being rude or was she uninformed? Was I insulted? I wasn't sure.

The second staff allowed as how "Tenere" was "some kind of new cologne they're pushing." And the third staff stopped adding eye shadow to her eye shadow and came over to join us. "Yeah," she said, "and it's g.w.p." (Because I am a consultant to retail stores, I happened to know that g.w.p. means "gift with purchase.")

That was the easy part.

Now, the pants.

Nobody had seen them. One suggested I try down-stairs. One suggested I try upstairs, on the second floor. The g.w.p. lady said they might be in Designer Collections.

This conversational encounter group and I were standing at the very first counter in the store, about fifteen feet from the big, big window, and there were six more mannequins wearing six more pairs of exactly the same pants on six display ledges right above our heads.

I persevered. I went downstairs.

"I don't know."

I went upstairs.

"Sorry. I don't know."

I asked in Lifestyles.

"I wish I knew. They sound great!"

I toured through Japanese pants, I visited Armani-Yohji-Gaultier-Ferre pants and private label pants, and I visited all the salespeople in every department asking them about the pants in the window.

Nobody knew nothin'.

After a while, a perky department manager appeared and said to me, "I'm sorry you are having so much trouble. Let me see if I can help you find those pants."

Alarms went off. A person who cared!

This event should be declared a National Retail Holiday!

She called the one department I hadn't yet visited.

No pants.

A stockman said he was just a stockman and didn't know anything at all.

She called the buyer. The buyer had no idea what pants she was talking about.

But then the perky person had an inspiration! She beeped the Display Department.

Two minutes later she hung up the telephone, flushed

with answers, victory, and customer service. She had reached the Display Department and found the explanation. She was no less pleased than Miss Marple is at the end of an Agatha Christie story.

"Those pants don't look like that at all," she said. "The effect was created by the Display Department. They pin them in at the ankles, they bunch up the extra pleats. The belt is from Women's Accessories and wouldn't fit you at all. Those are Union Bay pants and they're down in the basement. Come on down with me and I'll show you right where they are."

We went back down to the basement to find the pants. No pants. They were out of them. The Display Department had taken them all for display.

She started apologizing again, but I didn't stay to listen. For all I know, she may, to this day, still be standing there in front of the store on the "Tenere!" carpet, right in front of the sculpture next to the window with all those pants that were not for sale because they were on display.

Good service means *never* having to say, "I don't know."

Employees should never have to say "I don't know," but even if they do have to, they shouldn't. To the customer, "I don't know" is the same as "I don't care." The worst admission service providers should ever allow themselves to make is "Wait just a moment! I'll find out."

There are department stores I know that tell employees things on a "need to know" basis. I think employees need to know everything. People working without information are automatically demeaned and demoted, and can only feel hostile in addition to being completely unequipped because they are uninformed. Customers want information, and they disrespect and even distrust the person who is supposed to have it but doesn't.

I was stunned at Charivari to find a white shirt imported from Italy that had a price tag of $840. So I turned to a vacant but fashionable human being who was standing next to the shirt and asked for information. "Why is this shirt $840?" I asked, to which he replied, "I'm damned if I know!"

"There shouldn't be anything happening in the company that the front-line people don't know about," says Stew Leonard, Jr. Because of its notoriety, the store gets a lot of visitors, sometimes groups of them lugging cameras and notepads. The Leonards make sure everybody who works in the store knows who is there and why.

"If a customer comes into the store and sees people walking around shooting pictures, when she gets to the cash register, if she says to the cashier, 'Hey, what's goin' on over there?' we don't want the cashier to say, 'I don't know, nobody told me,' " says Stew Jr. "We try to get as much information out to them as we can.

"Every day we publish all our customer suggestions. We lay stacks of them on the table in the employee cafeteria so everyone can read them. We share the sales information, labor and profit information, expense information."

A few days after Sears inaugurated its "sale that never ends" pricing policy in 1989, a friend of mine went into one of their stores to buy a cordless electric screwdriver. He knew what he wanted to do, but he wasn't sure which cordless electric screwdriver he needed. He found six models, ranging in price from about $15 to about $60. Only two models had price tags, and only a couple of models had descriptive labeling. When he finally found a salesperson, the clerk didn't know and couldn't explain the differences.

"This is obviously a big problem and I think it is the area where Sears is going to win or lose with its new strategy," says author Don Katz. "The stores are going to have an assortment of goods that is narrower than before and it will include brand name merchandise and the store clerks are going to have to know about all this stuff. Instead of twenty-five trash compactors, they'll have only six. But the salespeople will have to know what is the difference between a Kenmore and a GE.

"Sears is finally getting the idea that *knowledge* is the best customer service right now. The customer is more knowledgeable and what you need to know to make a purchase these days, especially something technical, is mind-boggling.

"The customer is getting fed up with all the games they have to play to get the best price. Some of the sleazier retailers have been pulling this stuff about, 'If you bring the ad in showing the lower price . . .'

"It turns out these retailers can go to a manufacturer like Toshiba and say, 'Make this television for me at X price and make it exactly the same as you do for everybody else, but instead of a black case put a brown case on it.' That way Toshiba can put a different serial number on it and say it's not the same product, and the retailer can say the same thing to the customer. It may be the same item inside, but the discounter won't honor the 'lower advertised price' promise because the serial number isn't the same. Meanwhile the customer is already in the store."

Good information sells merchandise. Descriptions need to be as clear, and as persuasive, as the copy in a Lands' End catalog. Here is a compelling Lands' End headline:

"5 REASONS YOU SHOULD BUY OUR SUPER-T
INSTEAD OF AN ORDINARY T-SHIRT"

Is that direct enough for you? Have you ever met a "live" salesperson who was as good as that?

Every detail helps convince the customer to buy, without pressure, but with plenty of information.

1. T-shirts are prone to rip at the neck and shoulder seams because of the rough treatment and frequent launderings they usually have to endure. So we tape the neck and shoulder seams inside with soft SUPER-T fabric to prevent rip-outs at stress points. Taped seams give you chafe-free comfort inside the shirt too.

2. If you've had it with flimsy t-shirts, here's your answer! Our 100% cotton jersey is one of the heftiest t-shirt fabrics we know of, so it stands up to hard use. And it's engineered to resist shrinkage, so it keeps its fit after many washings and wearings.

3. We offer both short and long sleeves, so you can wear your SUPER-T in any season, for all kinds of activities.

4. Here's one more detail you wish every t-shirt had: a breast pocket to hold glasses, pens, whatever. And we reinforce the top corners so they won't give out on you.

5. When you wear your SUPER-T untucked, you'll be glad we finished the side vents with single needle stitching so your shirttails look neat!

Every Brookstone store has a sign in front which says, WHAT KIND OF STORE IS THIS? and then it tells you that Brookstone sells unusual and high-quality gadgets. Each gadget is displayed in a square modular box, and at the bottom of each box is a complete description of the product. Visually you can look at only one item and one description at a time, which is extremely good presentation, which translates into good service. The description is absolutely without exception the right description for the item in front of you, as in a museum.

This is harder to do with soft goods. You can do a pretty good job of merchandising a women's wraparound skirt or children's overalls the way Lands' End or Spiegel does. But you cannot put a dress in a box and describe it. What you can do is create garment tags that are in good, clear English and that tell you things you need to know to make a decision. A good garment tag is a good, silent salesperson. You can attach the tag somewhere obvious so that it is not hanging halfway down inside of the dress or the shirt. You can make it easy to tell if it is the price tag, the manufacturer's tag, or the inventory control tag, so that when the customer finally finds a tag it's not just a string of meaningless numbers.

Garment tags should be simple and they should tell you something about the garment, what it's made of, how to care for it, what it might coordinate with, the price, the size, and maybe some information about the manufacturer or the designer.

Units, a relatively new chain of women's clothing stores, does this fairly well. The store takes a piece of clothing and tells you how to wear it four different ways. That's service.

Good information is good service.

DEALING WITH DISASTER

Disasters can often breed triumphs. When things go wrong, you're on the right track if you seize the opportunity to convert the problem into better customer service. As

Harry S. Truman said, "When life hands you a lemon, make lemonade."

Customers often hand providers lemons. A customer handing you a lemon is causing a crisis. In written Chinese, the character representing the word for *crisis* is made up of two characters. One stands for "danger" (that's what most people think a crisis is), but the other stands for "opportunity."

When we added the fiftieth state, Albert Myers was stuck with thousands of forty-nine-star flags in his Illinois stores.

Most retailers would have whined and marked them down and lost money, but not Albert. He sold them all —at regular price—as collector's items. Disasters clobber mediocre people, but fighters find the opportunity.

Forbes magazine sent a reporter to follow a man who is paid by McDonald's to act like a customer. He goes into any McDonald's, unannounced, to sample the service. He checks out the french fries, spills orange juice, compliments helpers. He'll then go into the kitchen and announce that he works for McDonald's and couldn't help noticing that the right side of this McMuffin is lower than the left side, and he'll ask how that happened, and what can be done about it?

Even though they are all franchised operations, discipline matters, and this man and others work in their customer costumes to help keep the standards high.

Manager-critics acting like customers swarm through Disneyland right along with the rest of us, only they are more critical. They jot down notes, look for peeling paint, and mingle in the same experiences customers have. Then, when they've got a notebookful, they start fixing things. Disneyland "ain't broke," but they fix it constantly.

Domino's, the world's largest pizza delivery chain, has an effective way to measure customer satisfaction.

It pays ten thousand "mystery customers" $60 each to buy twelve pizzas throughout the year at any of its five thousand units, and to evaluate their quality and service. Manager compensation is based in part on these results.

The managers at Northwestern Mutual Life Insurance Co. rely on their customers to coach them. Each year, five policyholders descend on company headquarters in Milwaukee to tell the insurer what it is doing right and wrong. They have done this since 1907. Nothing and no one is off limits. The group's review is printed, unedited, in the company's annual report.

British Airways does not encourage crises, but it uses an electronic suggestion box that reports passenger problems as quickly as possible. The company placed a "video box," which is a seat in an enclosed booth facing a camera, in Heathrow International Airport. Passengers are invited to sit in the box and spout off about British Airways. The company plays these tapes back to its employees.

"It's rapid feedback—sometimes captured within moments of the service experience—and therefore more spontaneous and complete," says Michael Bruce. "Also, because it is essentially anonymous, it seems very honest. We also run forums where we have customers come in and tell us what they think about us. Our cabin crews also gather information from passengers, using a checklist of questions. Then they will sometimes have a session after the flight at the hotel with the marketing people. It's much more valuable than using researchers who don't fly. You can learn a lot listening to the front-line staff.

"They do something similar at Marks and Spencer, a London department store chain. They will put out a new line of shirts and use the shop attendants as a data resource, asking them what the customers are saying about it, how is the product moving. This has a very positive impact on front-line staff as well. They feel much more a part of the organization rather than just being there to take people's money."

Donald Hess is president of Parisian Department Store—but he personally attends to customer mail. "When we get letters from customers, if it's positive, I write back. If it's a complaint I call them immediately, or someone who can deal with that problem will call them immediately. We never let them go. It's the only way we can learn. It's our *friends* who take the time and make the effort to write us.

"This also sends a message to our sales associates. You can't make your people be nice to a customer when they come to return something, if the associate knows they could lose their job if they make an adjustment or violate a policy. Nobody at Parisian ever lost their job for doing what they thought was right for the customer or to make that customer happy."

Customers want the person they talk to to have the *authority* to help them handle their problem. A British Airways customer survey showed that customers easily tolerate a company's making a mistake, for example, losing a reservation. But when they come for help, they want the person who serves them to be able to work with them to find a way to rectify the situation.

Walter Geier, a business consultant, once asked a successful businessman for the secret to his success. Geier said the businessman replied

I take all the customers nobody else wants. I go out of my way to get the complainers, the tough customers, the ones who are never satisfied, the ones who keep demanding more and scream bloody murder when they don't get it. These are the best customers to have. For one thing, they've been around; they appreciate good service when they get it. And they know how rare it is. So they stay with you. They don't go running off the first time someone else dangles a special deal in front of them.

Also, their friends know how hard they are to please. So they tend to follow them, to take their advice and recommendations.

This supplies me with a steady supply of new customers. Also, by sounding off, they teach me things about what customers like and dislike, what they think is important. But most of all, they keep me and my employees on our toes; they won't let us get careless or overconfident for a moment.

Stew Leonard, Jr., says, "Once a month we have what we call a communication meeting with every department, formatted like a focus group. The manager starts out for fifteen minutes talking about the state of the department: sales, labor, profit, expenses, safety things, anything that's going on. After that he goes around the room and asks everybody, 'How is your job, what bugs you, what can I do to make it better?' We love the big complainers because they really get things going. The people who work in each department know how to improve things better than anybody else.

"I like the people who tell me what I'm doing wrong, who offer suggestions and keep coming up with ideas for improvement. I heard a statistic that one of the great Japanese companies gets over twenty ideas per employee per year. They are out there asking their employees how to improve their company. That's what we do in these communication meetings.

"But you have to act on these suggestions. The worst thing in the world is to ask people for ideas and suggestions and then ignore them. No idea is a dumb idea, even when you're sitting there with your people and one of them says, 'We should go out and buy a car wash and put it right outside the front door so all our customers can drive through it and get their cars washed, too.' The person sitting next to him thinks to himself, 'Boy, what a stupid idea. Watch Stew jump all over this guy.'

"Instead, what happens is I build it into a potentially good idea. I'll say, 'That's interesting, what makes you think of that?' 'Well,' they say, 'the parking is such a problem that maybe it would be nice to do something extra for the customers.' I might say, 'Well, we've got that property across the street. Maybe we could put a car wash across the street.' And they say, 'Hey, yeah. That's an idea.' And I say, 'Great, thanks.' And I write it down.

"The guy thinks, 'Hey, at least he listened to my idea.' It's not that I have to build a car wash. The main thing is I'm not squishing the little spark of energy that came from that person. No idea is a bad idea. As long as the person comes up and offers the idea, it's positive."

The Leonards write up what happens in these meetings, print the minutes, and hand them out so everyone can see and comment on them. The minutes are entertaining to read and nothing is considered confidential. Employees get a chance to gripe about gristly roast beef, old tomatoes, grimy display cases, and broken ovens in the barbecue department. "We need knives," or "Sales are tracking about the same as last year in the produce department," or "Customers are asking how long a fresh turkey lasts. Please answer: 7 to 10 days," or "Jeannie bugs me," or "Rose has a bad attitude." They also get to pat each other on the back for extra work or a job well done.

One of the great things about service at Nordstrom or SAS or This End Up is that these companies have given their employees the power and the responsibility to satisfy customers. When the Nordstrom shoe salesman told the customer to bring in the year-old shoes he never wore because they pinched, he didn't have to find an assistant manager to get permission. He didn't have to go through channels. He didn't have to find out if it was "in the strategy." Instead, he exchanged the old shoes for new ones, immediately, at no cost to the customer.

Lazarus, the Columbus, Ohio, department store, had an unequivocal policy of refunding customers' money at any time for any reason. The problem was that the managers hadn't informed the sales staff of the policy and they hadn't empowered them to carry it out. One day Mr. Lazarus, the owner, overheard a salesperson saying to a customer, "We can't refund your money." Mr. Lazarus, who was very old, just about went psychotic when he heard this. He went over to the salesclerk and said, "Come with me."

"Who are you?" the clerk asked.

"I'm Fred Lazarus. Come with me, we're going outside."

They walked out the doors and across Broad Street. There old Mr. Lazarus turned around, pointed up, and said, "You see that water tower up there?" pointing to a huge water tower on the roof of his store which had written across it, in very large letters, LAZARUS.

"Now I'm going to tell you why you're going to give everyone their money back whenever they want it."

The clerk started to go on about how the woman wasn't deserving of her money back and Mr. Lazarus cut him short.

"Read me the name on that water tower."

"It says Lazarus," the clerk said.

"That's right," he said. "And that's my name, too. And the reason we're going to give her her money back is because it's *my* money."

Many service providers suffer from this misplaced sense of loyalty. They think they are protecting the company from conniving customers, which may seem noble at the time but is shortsighted and must be discouraged. In this case, the employees of Lazarus became informed through the mythology that Fred Lazarus created by dragging this person out of the store and making a fuss over a minor return. After that, nobody working at Lazarus had to ask about the store's return policy. They had all been empowered to make the customer happy, no matter what.

RECOGNITION

Customers want recognition.

Service providers want recognition, too.

Even managers want recognition.

Taxi drivers are the best examples. All they ever do is provide service to customers.

On September 9, 1989, a taxi driver turned to his passenger and said, "Read this." It was a framed letter signed by the mayor of New York designating him the most courteous cab driver in New York—and it was dated 1978. This man has been proud of this for eleven years.

Another time another driver handed me a tape deck and said, "Push PLAY." I did. He was singing. He said, "I wrote this song. Sinatra has an option on it."

I've never met anybody who wasn't motivated by recognition; people want to be recognized for themselves or for their work, and the more famous they are, the more they want it. People work for recognition; even if they do it anonymously, they want their efforts recognized. Why don't managers ever say "thank you" to their employees? Employees work for recognition, but managers forget to give it.

This is one of the major reasons that service people give bad service to their customers; they reflect the way they are treated by their bosses, and they pass it right on to their customers.

Why aren't all salespeople on commission? It's the best form of recognition, but many businesses are terrified of it. Name the companies you think are best. I bet they'll all be recognizing their employees with some form of reward based on performance.

Travel agents live that way. Nordstrom has always been that way. Their competitors are all researching and testing and funding and discussing and whining about commissions, but they're not *doing* it. All wholesale salespeople are on commission.

At Scandinavian Airlines, a group of cabin attendants agitated for permission to sell chocolates, perfumes, and other gift items on board. They were told they could try it so long as they accepted financial responsibility for making it work. They did, and according to Jan Carlzon, the company's president, "We made millions from this venture, and the attendants earned hefty commissions."

Abraham and Straus has shocked New York by providing excellent customer service. I rushed over to find out what was happening. "It's simple," one of the many salespeople told me. "We're on commission."

It's not that simple, but it is a factor which most stores choose to ignore. They have a whole litany of bad clichés to defend themselves, such as "The salespeople fight over customers," or sillier yet, "We can't afford it." The result is that salaried salespeople are completely uninformed about the state of sales in their own store, nor do they care, because they get paid regardless of their personal performance. I have never met a really excellent salesperson who could not tell you instantly—

and to the dollar—how much she or he was selling. And I have never met a successful wholesale product salesperson who wanted to be on salary. This argument has intelligent advocates on both sides, but the notion of paying people commission, as motivation, is strong.

Commission is not the only way, and sometimes it's not the right way. But if you don't do it, you'd better provide some other form of inspiration, or else your people will not be inspiring your customers.

The clean and cheerful FedEx man who delivers art to a dealer in Philadelphia one day announced to her, "We bought a couple of new planes today."

"That's nice," she said.

"Well, it's pretty important to me," he explained. "It means business is good, and what with our growing profit-sharing plan, my wife and I are now planning to buy our first house."

I went to Lord & Taylor on the day they finished a $1.8 million remodeling job on the main floor of its flagship store on Fifth Avenue. It looked grand and expensive, and it felt cold. It was all marble and hard, echoing surfaces. Behind a cosmetics counter stood a veteran saleslady looking very grim. We had a typical New York conversation.

"How do you like it?" I asked.

"How do I like what?" she asked, eyeing me suspiciously.

"All this," I said gesturing. "One million eight hundred thousand dollars' worth of brand-new flagship store remodeling."

"You want to know how I like it?" she asked. "Come back here."

I went behind the counter and she pointed at the floor, which was also marble and stretched to infinity in all its high-sheen glory.

"You know what it's like to stand on that all day long?" she asked. "My feet hurt and it's only eleven-thirty in the morning. They spent almost two million dollars redecorating this place and they couldn't give me a little rug to stand on."

Stew Leonard's is fanatical about recognition. "We spend a lot of time trying to catch people doing something right, and then we make a fuss about it. We have more than two hundred photos of everybody plastered all over the store, and color photos of the stars of the month," says Stew Jr.

"It's real corny but it works. We have pictures of all the department managers. We have 'Up the Ladder' pictures of people who have been promoted. A new employee comes in and sees a guy with a tie on and figures, 'I'll never get that far.' So we have a color photo of that guy with a ladder next to it showing that he started as a stock boy and showing his promotions as he went up the ladder.

"We do a lot of parties. We take the department people out to dinner during the course of the year. We end up paying more for labor than other places, but we feel it comes back to us in happy customers and productivity. We expect an awful lot out of everybody. Our product prices aren't higher than the competition. They might even be lower. But we do over three thousand dollars per square foot a year versus around two hundred dollars for the industry. We think the difference is our service."

Waldenbooks requested each of its one thousand store managers to write up and send us the story of their best sales. We suddenly had one thousand highly motivational selling stories that were far more intense than the examples in the training manuals because they came from the people who are face to face with customers. We published and circulated this powerful idea file. Every employee whose triumph was published in that book was recognized and celebrated, and they and everyone else who read about them were all motivated to do more!

I was tearing through Bloomingdale's one day when I caught an expression of absolute hatred on the face of one of the salespeople in the menswear section. I went over and asked her what was the matter, and she immediately said, "See that man over there?"

I saw a prototype. A fast, aggressive merchant looking urgent and holding a manila envelope.

"A manager?" I asked.

"Yeah," she said. "*My* manager. That son of a bitch used to say 'thank you.' "

If managers don't thank their own people, just possibly that's why service providers don't say "thank you" to their customers.

It's the basis of smart follow-up, but it almost never happens.

When did you last receive a valentine from your car salesman? Wouldn't you be dumbfounded if you got a Thank-you from your lawyer?

The doorman at the hotel in Hawaii who got those tickets for the Pro Bowl is on commission in the form of his tips. The assistant manager who said "No" is not. Maybe if she had had a chance to make a quick twenty bucks she might have found us those tickets. But she's going to get paid for saying "No," so why should she take the trouble to find out how to say "Yes"?

What does it take to give real customer service? Listen to an expert, Harry Hoffman, former president of Waldenbooks, who has a passion for Jaguar sports cars. He's owned four of them and was having his latest serviced one day when he got into a conversation with a salesman in the showroom about possibly buying a fifth. The salesman had promised to get him some additional details.

"I'm the kind of customer who is very susceptible

and I would have bought the Jaguar if the guy had just dropped me a note or phoned with any kind of follow-up information," Harry said. "But I heard nothing. A few weeks later I found myself in somebody else's showroom and I ended up buying a Porsche. That Jaguar salesman blew a forty-thousand-dollar sale."

This has to be the simplest thing in the world for a service provider to do, and hardly anyone does it. Libby Brown complains that even though she's bought three houses, numerous cars, four or five sizable boats, and other big-ticket items in her life, "No one has ever written me a thank-you note. The size of the purchase shouldn't matter. It should be done for everything.

"At This End Up, after you buy from us you'll get a handwritten note from the person who sold it to you, and the note should say something about your little boy enjoying his bunk beds or something personal. Once we deliver [the furniture] to you, hopefully within three days, you will receive a telephone call asking how our service was, how you are enjoying the product, and asking if there is anything else we might be ordering up for you. We try for one hundred percent. I doubt we make it. We measure it on our customer service questionnaires, thousands of which we send out every year. We try for even the ones who spend only ten dollars on a pillow."

The Campton Place Hotel in San Francisco, one of my favorite hotels, sends me a card thanking me every time I stay there. When I arrive, they send a little note up to my room welcoming me back and telling me that this is my tenth visit. When I was quoted in an article on retailing in the *Wall Street Journal*, Mr. Thorn, the hotel manager, sent me a note of recognition along with a copy of the article in case I missed it. Great service.

There is a scuba diving equipment store in Nevada that takes photos during each customer's dive. At Christmas they send you a card with the picture of you during your dive. It costs practically nothing and probably encourages customers to remember what a good time they had and to make reservations for next season.

The sale is the major moment of service, but the follow-up can be just as important and can have more impact.

Roy Dyment, a doorman at the Four Seasons Hotel in Toronto, neglected to load a departing guest's briefcase in his taxi. The doorman called the guest, a lawyer, in Washington, D.C., and found that he desperately needed the briefcase for a morning meeting. Dyment hopped on a plane and delivered the briefcase—without first getting approval from his boss. The company named Dyment "Employee of the Year."

WIMPS ABOUT TIPPING

Tipping is a form of recognition: a way for customers to say "thank you" to service providers.

Americans are really wimps about tipping. We tip for bad service, indifferent service, and every other kind of service, and we do it automatically. In Europe and Asia tipping is not expected, but good service *is*. In some Asian countries, a tip is an insult. Many establishments automatically add a service charge to the bill.

Just try not tipping in an American restaurant or taxicab. You will find out quickly that it is easier to tip than not to tip and put up with the consequences. This is the land of brandy snifters stuffed with dollar bills on bars and entertainment pianos, of nasty little notices saying EACH COAT $1.50 in hotel checkrooms, and of signs that say TIP BIG. I GOT A FAMILY staring you down on bulletproof taxi partitions.

A tip is not always money. American Airlines provides its frequent flyers with a novel and effective way of "tipping" for exceptional service. The program is called "You're SomeOne Special." Every three months American's AAdvantage passengers are mailed a set of four "You're SomeOne Special" coupons with a notice:

> As one of our most valued customers we are committed to providing you with exceptional service and the best way to do so is through our employees. Please help us recognize and reward those employees who make you feel good about flying American Airlines.
>
> Enclosed are four "You're SomeOne Special . . ." cards, each of which may be presented to any employee who has given you exceptional service. To reward someone with whom you have had direct contact—a ticket agent, for instance—just complete the information on the back of the card and present the card to the employee. To recognize an individual you do not see—a reservations representative, for example—just ask for the name, employee number, station and branch, complete the card and mail it to the address the employee suggests.

Accumulating these coupons enables employees to exchange them for confirmed reservations for themselves and their families, instead of waiting for standby space on flights. Whenever I've handed one to someone special at American, they have been genuinely pleased (and so have I by the service that made me want to do it). This program of "tipping" both encourages and recognizes excellent service. I fly American as often as possible.

At the Burswood Hotel and Casino in Perth, Western Australia, there is a "butler floor" which costs more and is worth it. The "more" that it costs is about as much as you'd tip for the services you get—if you could get them. You call on the services of your butler whenever you need an agent. Your butler will oversee your orders for room service, laundry, and shoe shining, will clean your room—whenever and as often as you leave it—and will watch over you with highly trained attention.

I was struggling to clean my filthy tennis shoes after a trek through the countryside, and I thought: here's a test, I'll ask my butler if he would do it for me. Thirty minutes after he carried off my shoes, the telephone rang.

"Hello, Mr. Glen. This is Johnny, your butler. I have finished washing and drying your athletic shoes. I am calling to inquire whether you would like me to do up the laces in the parallel manner, or whether you would like them crossed over."

And then the doorbell rang and Johnny presented me with my clean shoes, on a tray.

I had already paid for this service, but I tipped him some more. Wouldn't you?

Late that afternoon, I checked out and prepared to fly to Sydney. There was a paralyzing national airline strike, and the airports were disaster areas.

I needed information badly. At eleven-thirty P.M., after three hours of waiting without information, I approached the Ansett Airlines agent and asked how late this flight was going to be.

Airlines know everything, but they never tell you anything. Apparently, they don't feel they have to share any information with you, even though nowadays you can expect almost every plane in the world to be late.

Don't bother to call the airlines ahead of time from your home or office. You'll be on "hold" longer than it takes to get to the airport. Even when they do materialize on the telephone, they inevitably assure you that every flight they ever have is always arriving and departing on time, to the instant. So save your phone call.

When you arrive at the airport you will then of course, discover that your flight is late, but you will never know *how* late. But the airline knows the exact status of your incoming flight; they have to, so that its planes don't crash. But it does not make announcements, or update its television monitors, or offer alternative flights, and you mustn't hassle it with questions as it is busy giving *many* other people the same fine service it is giving you.

And so you sit there, aging, in view of the agent and the television monitor, just glad to be allowed to be there, humbly hoping for any old discarded scrap of information. You are grateful just for the occasional glance as you sit there, at their feet, a victim of cigarette smoke and babies being ill, suspended in total ignorance until the airplane you are waiting for suddenly bursts forth from the clouds, lands, and comes right up in front of you and stops.

When I finally got this Ansett agent's attention, I said, "Tell me when this flight is leaving!"

"Just sit down," he said. "You're lucky to get on any flight at all!"

That stunned me back into the real world of service. No service, no butlers, no tips, no heart . . . all in the same day, the same city, the same economy.

The next time you get lousy service, try giving the provider the "C" sign instead of a tip. This is a form of recognition that isn't money. And you will have money left over to really tip the people who deserve and earn it.

Or just go on tipping for nothing and getting it.

ALMOST FLAWLESS

Tiffany strides the corner of Fifth Avenue and 57th Street, New York, like a colossus. The mobs approach the fortress from around the world in high expectation, peering into the famous windows at the splendor within. Walk in: this is where energy meets money. It is very busy inside, but quiet, like a glittering casino suddenly minus the sound. Tiffany sparkles into the faces of the customer staring into cases where the wonders of the world are on display. They WANT it. The money flows in and out like the tides: the customers are smiling. Princesses and people who generally can't afford it stand there side by side, and none of them leave without buying something. Buying something at Tiffany reassures you, you've been to Tiffany, the best.

Except for the service. This is the tiny flaw in the otherwise perfect blue-white diamond. Close, but no cigar. Give Tiffany a 9.9 on the flawlessness scale.

The service is polite. A well-informed polite person will direct you to the third floor for anniversary gifts, china, and glass. But when you go up in the elevator with the woman in the smart, clean uniform, you can't help noticing as the elevator rises, that she is picking her nail polish off. A mere detail. You hope she'll get over it.

The elevator doors open onto third and Tiffany hits

you again. A panorama of crystal throws lights all over the room. They have it all, the best selection in the world. No matter how much you want to spend, there's enough here to enable you to concentrate until you make the right selection, the best. It will be wrapped with pride in the famous blue box with the famous white ribbon. The salespeople shuffle quietly back and forth, performing tasteful little errands on behalf of their customers. They make respectful inquiries as to whether you would like informed assistance, dealt out equally to cave men and kings. And there usually are a couple of kings sitting there ordering more than you ever thought of.

An announcement floats into the tinkling air. "Please make your selections. The store will close at five-thirty." You calculate how much time you've got. In Tiffany everyone has a wristwatch.

Try to imagine a silent stampede. There is a palpable quickening to the pace of the money piling up at the computer terminals behind the velvet doors. And finally you find two cut-crystal goblets so absolutely right that they can carry your love in a gift box.

You come to a decision. You know what you want, and you want it. You are ready to pay. Now is the time that the legendary Tiffany service goes into action.

The lady in the semi-Chanel suit comes back from the telephone and tells you they're out of them.

In the depths of Tiffany, at the heart of the reputation for dependability, constancy, good taste, and reassurance, they are out of them. The tasteful lady has entirely won your heart, and now she's stamping on it.

But she can order them. Fifteen dollars for Federal Express. U.P.S. will be $3.50. She'll check. She'll call the warehouse. This way, please, sir, please be seated (shuffle, shuffle, keep the customer quiet and out of the way).

You sit. She calls the warehouse. The warehouse is

closing. "I need a shelf count." Pause. "But it's just twenty minutes after five," she says into the telephone. She prevails. She reserves the glasses. She starts writing up the check.

"Before you finish that," you say, "why are you charging *me* for U.P.S.? I am perfectly ready to take the merchandise out of the store right now, but I cannot because you do not have the merchandise to give me. Why would you charge me extra for this service?"

That seemed a decent question. She said, "I'll have to ask the manager." She had evidently convinced the manager to invest $3.50 in this troublemaking customer on behalf of selling two extremely expensive goblets because she soon returned and primly said, "We will absorb the U.P.S. charge."

But you ask, "Would you have charged me for the U.P.S. if I had not asked?" And she said, "Yes."

So you save $3.50 by making a "C" sign at Tiffany. And Tiffany, almost flawless, falters in customer service and ends up a 9.9.

And so you somewhat sadly take the Tiffany elevator down to the main floor. As you descend, you see that the elevator operator has finished her nails and is now directing her attention, very discreetly, to her teeth. You remember that upstairs you had seen a display of solid silver toothpicks.

Management should really give these to the staff as Christmas gifts if they really don't mind them cleaning their teeth while they hang suspended in an elevator with their customers.

Back on the ground, you join the smiling masses of princesses and shahs and wondering midwesterners. Most of them are carrying large blue Tiffany shopping bags as we all pass through the portals of the almost-flawless Kingdom of Tiffany.

FILES OF STRANGENESS

Customers can be strange. They return furniture after seven years, claiming it is haunted.

A customer had owned a set of furniture for seven years, and now he wanted his $1,200 back from This End Up. The company has a lifetime guarantee on product quality and a "whimsy" guarantee which says you can return your purchase at any time for any reason at all.

"We'll take it back," the store manager said. "But if you don't mind telling me, what is the problem?"

"The furniture is haunted," the customer said.

"Say what?" the manager asked.

"Haunted."

"Why did it take you seven years to find out?" the manager asked.

"I thought it was our house that was haunted, but we've just moved to a new house and the furniture still moans and groans at night and we'd like you to take it back."

Libby Brown says, "This End Up once paid a two-hundred-dollar veterinary bill for someone who said the smell of the stain in the wood caused his bulldog to have a convulsion."

But This End Up employees have been known to go even further. An employee at one store was dispatched to a woman's home after she called to complain that a piece of furniture had been delivered unassembled and she could not put it together. When the employee got there he discovered that the woman had bought the furniture from Sears. But he assembled it for her anyway! That's great service.

All customers are not created equal. But salespeople prejudge them, and they often prejudge them wrong. I was standing in the Louis Vuitton shop at Saks one very rainy day when a man in a dreadful raincoat walked in. All of the clerks decided they wouldn't bother with him because he didn't look rich and his taste wasn't, well, Saks-like. They ignored him, but he stayed, so eventually one of them drifted over in his direction.

Within fifteen minutes this man had ordered fourteen pieces of Vuitton luggage—worth about $4,300. When the clerk checked "upstairs" he found the man had virtually unlimited credit. The clerk decided to uncoil and visit with his customer.

The customer then said, "My daughter also needs a wardrobe trunk." That freaked the clerk out, because he didn't even know if Vuitton made a wardrobe trunk. Somebody called France and found out that for $1,800 Vuitton made a wardrobe trunk. The customer said, "Okay, write it up."

As the clerk was writing up this additional order for this person who he had at first assumed was some impoverished refugee, he said, "I'm sure your daughter will just love all this luggage. Is she getting married?"

This customer had yet another surprise for the Saks clerk. "No," he said. "She's not getting married, she's nine years old. She's going to camp!"

Service providers should never say, "I wasn't hired to do that." There are as many ways to become a creative service provider as there are people who do it; it is a

highly individual matter and a continuing adventure. No
one will ever decide how it works once and for all.

Any job that asks you to be creative, and also pays
you for it, is one of the best jobs you can ever have.

The *best* guide to becoming a better service provider
will come from you yourself. You will find that the way
you deal with customer service is much the same way
you deal with life.

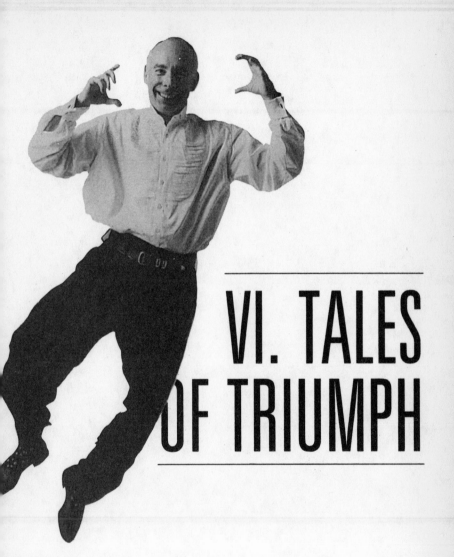

VI. TALES OF TRIUMPH

REVOLUTION IN SPOKANE

The revolution is on! Individuals are making the "C" sign right in the faces of service providers who are not doing what they want.

Customer John Barrier went into the Old National Bank (now U.S. Bank) in Spokane to cash a $25 check. On his way out of the parking lot, the kid in the booth told him he would have to charge him sixty cents or he would have to take his parking ticket back inside to get it validated.

John Barrier reparked his pickup, reentered the bank still wearing his Acme Concrete Co. baseball cap, and re-presented himself to the teller who had cashed his check. She informed him that she could not validate his ticket; validations were given only for "transactions" and the policy of the bank was that check cashing was not a "transaction."

"Let me be sure I heard that correctly," said the customer. "You will not validate my sixty cent parking ticket?" "You heard correctly," said the teller.

John said, "Get me the manager."

"Okay," said the clerk, "but he'll just tell you the same thing I did."

The manager "emerged," as managers sometimes do in times of trouble, and told the customer that as he understood it, the teller had already told him the bank's policy, and that the bank would not validate his parking ticket because he had not made a transaction.

Only then did John Barrier, the customer, make the "C" sign at the manager. "I am about to make a transaction," he said. "Give me the one million dollars I keep in your bank. I'm taking it next door."

And that is exactly what he did. He deposited his million dollars in the bank right next door, where his parking ticket was cheerfully validated.

This multimillionaire real estate developer, who didn't quite look the part, had a genuine customer triumph. And the Old National Bank saved sixty cents.

OVER THERE

But a bank can also have a triumph, and here is a tiny one that will bring tears to your eyes.

The world's biggest bank, Dai-Ichi Kangyo Bank of Tokyo, provides a memorable service to its customers.

Down in the bowels of the Dai-Ichi Kangyo Bank in Tokyo are the safety deposit box rooms.

This is a pristine place of polished marble and spotless stainless steel. On the marble desk where customers sign to get the key to their box, there is a lovely lacquer tray holding six pairs of eyeglasses, of various prescriptions, to assist you in case you forgot your own and wish to read some small print.

That's a tiny, but important, triumph.

TOAST AND TRIUMPH

The best scene ever played in the service revolution is the famous diner scene in the 1970 film *Five Easy Pieces*. Jack Nicholson, a strange customer if ever there was one, spars with a brittle, bleached, grim waitress over an order of toast. When the film was first released, audiences nearly rioted in sympathy with the heroic role that Nicholson portrayed as a harried customer fighting for service. Nicholson makes a violent "C" sign at a classic "It's not my department" waitress:

NICHOLSON: I'd like a plain omelette, no potatoes—tomatoes instead—a cup of coffee and wheat toast.

WAITRESS: (*Pointing to the menu with her pencil*) No substitutions.

NICHOLSON: What do you mean? You don't have any tomatoes?

WAITRESS: Only what's on the menu. You can have a plain omelette. It comes with cottage fries and a roll.

NICHOLSON: I know what it comes with but it's not what I want.

WAITRESS: (*Disgusted*) I'll come back when you make up your mind.

NICHOLSON: Wait a minute. I *have* made up my mind. I'd like a plain omelette, no potatoes on the plate. A cup of coffee and a side order of wheat toast.

WAITRESS: (*Her face tightening*) I'm sorry. We don't have any side orders of toast. English muffins or a coffee roll.

NICHOLSON: What do you mean you don't make side orders of toast? You make sandwiches, don't you?

WAITRESS: Would you like to talk to the manager?

NICHOLSON: You've got bread, and a toaster of some kind?

WAITRESS: I don't make the rules.

NICHOLSON: Okay, I'll make it as easy for you as I can. I'd like an omelette—plain—and a chicken salad sandwich on wheat toast, no mayonnaise, no butter, no lettuce, and a cup of coffee.

WAITRESS: (*Writing*) A number two. Chicken sal sand. Hold the butter, the lettuce, the mayonnaise, and a cup of coffee. (*Sarcastically*) Anything else?

NICHOLSON: Yeah. Now all you have to do is hold the chicken, bring me the toast, give me a check for the chicken salad sandwich and you haven't broken any rules.

WAITRESS: You want me to hold the chicken, huh?

NICHOLSON: I want you to hold it between your knees.

WAITRESS: (*Turning to point to a sign that says "We Reserve the Right to Refuse Service"*) You see that sign, sir? Yes, you all have to leave.

I'm not taking any more of your smartness and sarcasm.

NICHOLSON: You see this sign? (*Sweeps all the water glasses off the table and storms out*)

That film was shot over twenty years ago, but it could still be tomorrow in America. Audiences cheered, but they didn't act. It wasn't happening to them.

THE CAPPUCCINO AND THE ROSE

Heaven can cost you just three dollars.

There must be hundreds of little coffee bars amongst the skyscraper shopping centers in Tokyo.

You don't expect much from a cup of coffee at a counter, and it is a slightly strange idea to order cappuccino in Japan. But one day three of us did that anyway.

First, the waitress brought us three cups of ordinary black coffee. Just as we were beginning to think she hadn't understood what we had ordered, she held up her hand in a gesture meaning "please wait."

She came right back with three silver spoons on three plates. In each spoon was a sculpture of a rosebud made of whipped cream. She lowered each spoon, one at a time, into each cup of coffee. When the teaspoon hit the heat, the whipped cream rosebud opened. It blossomed into a full-blown rose. It lived about four seconds, then dissolved and spread out across the coffee.

Three cups of cappuccino!

Three dollars.

Wouldn't it be great if another million service providers cared that much? And then another few million customers would remember their experiences forever? But we are slow. Americans just keep whining and wanting things to get better.

We wish that Exxon had not infected Alaska, but we don't want to fight about it. We can't afford to wait, but we're still reluctant to fight about it.

The revolution *is* coming. We can all help make it happen sooner, and we can make it an American-led revolution *if* customers and service providers are willing to fight for it. Otherwise, the Japanese and the Koreans and the British and the Swedes will be happy to do it for us and take the rewards.

INTERNATIONAL "C" SIGNS

Triumphs of customer service are a habit in some other countries. You expect the Orient Express to be a triumph.

You expect a Rolex watch to work and an Italian meal to be excellent.

We are astonished, but not entirely surprised, when the laundry at the Oriental Hotel in Bangkok packs each lowly sock and *T*-shirt separately in a plastic bag, nestles the bag in a cardboard box, wraps the box in gift paper and ties it with ribbons and orchids. Wasteful! Ridiculous! Unnecessary!

So is Love!

One of life's biggest challenges is getting service in France—if you are an American. I still have a copy of a letter written to me by the three-star restaurant Taillevent in Paris, declining to accept my three-months-in-advance dinner reservation on the grounds that the restaurant had a policy of no longer accepting reservations from Americans.

I now *needed* to go to Taillevent. So, I got an agent. (Obviously, someone French. Maybe they'd take it from him.) I called the concierge at my Paris hotel, told him I would be staying there three nights, and I wanted to go to Taillevent on one of them. I would leave it to him.

We three got to Paris, and on the big day we skipped lunch (a very difficult maneuver in Paris), took long aromatic baths, got really dressed, and went to the restaurant.

It wasn't just the food and the service, it was the total experience, from the instant the front door swung open just before we reached for it, through the uninterruptive disappearance of every spilled crumb or the unintrusive genuine guidance in selecting the best of the best from the best, until we had eaten a meal so good we were giddy.

Drifting slightly, the three of us rose as our three chairs glided out from beneath us, and we three stepped out into the reception area, where, to our astonishment, three ladies stood waiting, holding our three coats open to help us into them. How did they know our individual coats—all three black—or when we would be getting up from dinner, or when to appear in front with them at exactly that moment?

That's just the way it is in the best restaurant in the world.

That's service.

But I couldn't resist giving them the "C" sign. I got out the letter of refusal they had sent me, and handed it to the host as he was bowing us back out into the cruel, hard world. He smiled graciously and said nothing. He is, after all, French.

A triumph for both the restaurant *and* for the customer. We got in, but we wouldn't have without a "C" sign. We needed to cause it to happen. So do you.

PARADISE UNPOSTPONED

The Regent Hotel begins the minute you get to Hong Kong. A conspicuously uniformed chauffeur is at the gate in the airport, holding an exquisitely scripted sign with your name on it. You are relieved of your carry-ons and your luggage tags, floated through customs, and escorted to the car, and you depart. Another gent has gone to get your luggage, and you'll see it next unpacked in your room at the hotel.

The car is a Rolls-Royce, and although you are dimly aware of one of the world's most exotic cities whizzing quietly by outside your windows, you really concentrate instead on how comfortable you are, and how you just skipped forty uncivilized insults in the airport; no luggage, no waiting, no money exchange, no taxi lines, and no dirty cars.

You reach your hotel too soon, a thing that has never happened before, and a thousand doors swing open. First, the door of the Rolls; then you see the welcoming hand of the majordomo clearing your path to the big front doors, which little boys in uniforms are swinging inward as you mount three glistening marble steps. Inside, a manager awaits you, gesturing towards the elevator doors, which are being held back for your approach.

The inside of the elevator is upholstered, but before you reach to feel the leather, more doors, more managers—the pace picks up; you're almost at your room. The door is open. Three more smiling faces wait inside your room. You are offered three silver platters: one with hot tea in a lacquered cup and an orchid, one with chocolates arranged in pyramid form, and one with fresh fruit set on palm leaves in the shape of a bird of paradise. Paradise! This entire sequence takes just twenty minutes.

It is impossible to exaggerate in describing the service.

They anticipated everything and I asked for nothing.

All of the Regent is like that, believe it or not. The little white-uniformed lady who pushed the silent broom around the marble floors at frightening speed, always smiling, never sweeping a guest, but always polishing the marble where you walk, the waiter who pours your house wine in the coffee shop with laser-beam intensity, but smiling; the waiters in the world-class restaurant, Plume, practice polishing plates before setting them down before guests. They do this like a fine ballet troupe warm-up, every afternoon for an hour, for as long as they are employed. This cast of thousands, those who provide and never need to be asked for anything; they are all making the "C" sign on behalf of every guest.

Call them guests. Call them whatever you like, but they all like the Regent.

Someone put more postcards into your writing set after observing you had used two of them. They did it since breakfast, silently, anticipating the chance, however small, that you might be inspired to write another postcard after lunch.

Make a reservation in the health club. A complete black marble suite is yours alone. You get black marble walls and floors and a circular black marble whirlpool bath with black marble faucets carved like shells. You have a shower made of a single piece of black marble, including the seat. There's a sauna and a massage table under a retractable ceiling sun machine, oak buckets full of brushes for your back rub, fifty towels, two terry cloth bathrobes, and a long black marble shelf lined with costly balms and unguents. There are people to help you if you want them. You will be rubbed and scrubbed and tanned and washed and dried and you will smell good and spend a lot of money. You are the customer.

Eventually, the car is waiting to take you to the airport, and you could swear you see them brushing back the tears as you go bye-bye.

AIRLINE "C" SIGN

British Airways canceled a flight from Hong Kong to London, thereby dumping its passengers into the Kai Tak Airport until they could schedule everybody onto another airline. The next British Airways flight to London was in forty-eight hours, so they tried to put their passengers on some other flight as soon as possible.

But one tough customer sat in the airport refusing to be transferred. She wanted to travel on British Airways, not another airline. She was making a different kind of "C" sign. She announced that she would wait until the next British Airways flight went to London. British Airways decided to honor her reservation.

The plane being repaired had to get to London eventually anyway. And so this passenger waited out the delay, and then flew nonstop from Hong Kong to London as the only passenger on a 747, except for the crew and twenty-three flight attendants. British Airways was wise enough to send out a press release, and the story flashed around the world.

IT IS MY DEPARTMENT

If you and I were working together, and you gave me one hour to convince you of the value of service in America, we would use that hour at Stew Leonard's.

We would not be the first people there. Stew Leonard's has been written about and talked about, and hordes of people not their regular customers trek up to Connecticut to see the store and to spend money. Many of these pilgrims are would-be service providers. In great anticipation they head up the highway to the shrine. They go, they see, they understand the mysteries, they have fun, and they get ideas—probably more ideas than from anywhere else they've been.

But when they get home and the mystical glow dies down, routine returns to do its ugly work, and then, eventually, they all slow down, and sigh, and say, "It's not my department."

Nobody can motivate you but you. The word *motivate* means "to move." Nobody can make you act except you. Stew Leonard's (or Disneyland or Federal Express) can inspire you, but it will not move you to action.

So come with me. Here's a little trip to Stew Leonard's in the hope that ideas will stir you to action.

The store started life as a family dairy in 1937. It is still a family dairy store. But let's get right to the point: with 33,000 square feet of selling space, it does over

$100 million in sales each year. That's $3,030 per square foot, per year, or more than fifteen times the national average of just over $200 per square foot.

The Leonard family has the ability to make every employee responsible. They try to make everyone believe that *everything* is every employee's department.

Jodie, who picks up the phone when you call, is entirely responsible for the first impression you might ever have of Stew Leonard's.

Jodie is terrific.

Most grocery stores in America do not have listed telephone numbers. You cannot call them. They do not want to talk to you.

The first afternoon I ever went to Stew Leonard's I saw the following thirty-seven ideas in action:

- a petting zoo to calm the nerves of you and your children after it takes you too much time to park because of the traffic jam in the parking lot. You are defused.

- a "one idea" bus which takes employees on regular trips to interesting businesses in search of ideas to put into action back home.

- a person dressed as a chicken at the front door waving and nodding as you approach. If you ask the chicken, "Why are you dressed as a chicken?" the chicken whispers, "We aren't supposed to talk"!

- the famous six-thousand-pound rock that you have to walk around to get into the store. These words are chiseled on it:

RULE 1: THE CUSTOMER IS ALWAYS RIGHT.

RULE 2: IF THE CUSTOMER IS EVER WRONG, REREAD RULE 1.

- a store designed with only one continuous aisle, which takes you from the entrance to the cashiers. You can go forward or backward in this aisle. There are no other aisles. You are comfortably guided past every item in the store.

- eight hundred items in the store. Most supermarkets stock twenty-five thousand items and confuse the customer, and lose sales because of it.

- very, very, very large shopping carts.

- a computer that monitors ten-item display platforms at strategic spots around the store. The computer tracks the sales of the single items piled high on each platform. The computer is checked once an hour. *If the rate of sale for any one item falls below projections in that time, the item is changed.* This keeps the store in touch with what its customers are buying, every sixty minutes.

- the world's fastest mechanical egg-laying chicken.

- customer egg selection: you can select your own eggs and put them into cartons. These cartons hold eighteen eggs instead of twelve. Most people decide to buy eighteen. (This idea has been discontinued. The crowds at the display were blocking traffic.)

- a spotless dairy entirely visible behind walls of glass. School kids are learning; someone from the *Wall Street Journal* is making notes.

- Hank and Beau, two robot cows that moo at you from a bridge above your head.

- an immense sign across the entrance to the bakery that proclaims WELCOME! WE'RE GLAD YOU CAME!

- a personnel manager, for the month of December, handing out delicious cookies to customers waiting in line. (Can you believe that?)

- an employee's pizza recipe, which is now a best-selling item in the store.

- pistachio nuts. Stew Sr. didn't think they would sell, but

Stew Jr. did. When his father went to Florida, Stew got a lot of pistachios, put them out, sold them all, and showed the results to his father. (Leonard's now sells a ton a week.)

- a sign, met frequently: SUCCESSFUL PEOPLE ARE THE FEW WHO FOCUS IN AND FOLLOW THROUGH—STEW LEONARD. (Motivation—out in the store! Whom is Stew talking to?)

- a photographer who roams the store with a Polaroid camera, looking for babies. When he sees one, he gets permission from its mother, snaps its picture, and hands the picture to the mother.

- photographs. They pave the walls. There are photographs of Employees of the Month going back years, not just one employee in one frame for a month, to be torn out and replaced. Photos of graduating seniors at Norwalk High School. Shots of Paul Newman introducing his own products in the store. Of Frank Perdue, who sold about one-half the chickens on the East Coast, and who sold more to Stew than any other account. And photos of customers—a wall of them. The "Wall of Fame" has thousands of pictures of Stew Leonard's customers carrying Stew Leonard's shopping bags from the Coral Sea to the Vatican. Each photo brought three dollars as a reward. And photos of King Kong, Neil Armstrong, and Ronald Reagan, all carrying Stew Leonard's shopping bags.

- a bulletin board full of Christmas cards—from customers.

- a huge display with a picture of Stew saying, "WE WANT YOU HAPPY! Please! Please! Let us know anytime you're not satisfied."

- a suggestion box for both customers and staff which is emptied every morning. Every suggestion is answered before eleven A.M. Sometimes these answers are hand-delivered to customers with a dozen cookies fresh from Stew Leonard's bakery. About fifty suggestions a day come from employees. In Japan the average employee submits twenty-five suggestions per year, while in the United States the average is 0.14 per person, per year.

- a mail box, photo developing, and lots of telephones for customers.

- a sign on the pay phone in the store that says, MORE PHONES BY REGISTER #1.

- checks bounced by customers posted on a display board with a notice: WE LEARNED THE HARD WAY.

- security personnel dressed as sheriffs

- a wall behind the scenes, in the employee's area, with forty pictures of things Stew Jr. saw, didn't like, and took pictures of one morning when he got up and went into the store at three-thirty A.M. He put them all up on the wall under a huge sign that said, IS THERE A MANAGER IN THE HOUSE? The employees didn't like it either! But in doing this, Stew had not only broken his routine but everyone else's, too, and they all had a fresh start to a new day. And what was more, the messes were cleaned up instantly.

- a more effective method of slicing cold cuts.

- a far more efficient sugar dispenser in the employee cafeteria.

- the warehouse manager's office decorated for Christmas —by his employees.

- one book—*The Life of Walt Disney*—on Stew Sr.'s desk.

- advertising—but not about groceries: "MERRY CHRISTMAS TO ALL OUR CUSTOMERS," "CONGRATULATIONS TO THE NORWALK HIGH SCHOOL GRADUATES."

- employee newspaper, called *Stew's News* (of course!).

- an employee meeting every Thursday about "How can we have more fun?"

- the store philosophy: "To make the customer say 'Wow!' "

- wherever possible, employees on individual quotas. Employees know how much they have to do and they know how they are doing. Complete information is their department.

- a sign on the back of the doors that employees go through before they go into the store to meet customers:

    IF YOU SEE SOMEONE WITHOUT A SMILE,
    GIVE THEM ONE OF YOURS!

There was more, much more, but far more remarkable was *how these things got done.*

The real genius of Stew Leonard's is not ideas, but *action.* You can easily find out *what* Stew Leonard's does, but the magical mystery is that it *does* it. That is the part the students of service may not realize, as they cruise the aisles with laser vision, looking for ideas.

These ideas came from customers and employees and from Stew Leonard and his passionate family.

They came from everywhere, and the Leonards listen and *act.*

The Leonard family is motivated. The Leonards would rather be doing what they do than anything else. They love their employees. They love their customers. They love groceries and their salad bar. They love their business and their community and the world.

The Leonards believe that everything is everyone's department. The family has offices upstairs, but they do not believe that any hour up there can ever compare with an hour down on the floor with customers and staff. So that's where you usually find them, trying to make every employee believe that *everything* is his or her department, too. They demonstrate. They get ideas. They respond. They make decisions. They have fun. They are enthusiastic, dramatic, slightly weird. They are *in the store.*

They get themselves and their staff and the customer to motivate themselves.

They all feel, "This is my store!" And in that blissful state you never hear the dreaded incantation, "It's not my department!"

IN PRAISE OF INDIVIDUALS

Revolutions are begun by individuals. That's the way revolutions begin.

There isn't much of a service revolution going on in America in the government, or in big groups, or in corporations, or in systems. But there are individuals in all those places, and their revolution is already under way. Each triumph is a small one, but the triumphs add up, and these individuals' futures are filled with possibilities.

We have a school system which puts our national literacy level just ahead of Swaziland, but there are individual teachers like Jaime Escalante who are creating greatness. The movie *Stand and Deliver* (get it, watch it, and rejoice) is the real story of this calculus teacher and his eighteen high school students in East Los Angeles. This is a part of the world where many consider even the idea of education to be hopeless.

In the movie, Escalante is trying to serve his students

by educating them and giving them hope and a future, but the service provider, the Educational Testing Service, is so skeptical of the results earned by Escalante's students that they are investigated for cheating. The testing service is not ready to believe that a great teacher could produce great minds in East L.A. Escalante and his students don't fight bloodily. Instead, they stay and fight persistently until it is established that they passed their exams legitimately. A great teacher teaching is surely a service of love.

A small triumph began at Waldenbooks when a man who had never been in a Waldenbooks, didn't like to read, and was just frantic because he had only an hour to find a birthday present for his mother, became entangled in a display rack. In his efforts to free himself he tore the leg of his pants. He was thoroughly irritated.

The store manager immediately called up the regional manager who suggested that the guy go next door, buy a reasonably priced pair of pants, and bring back the receipt, and Waldenbooks would supply him the birthday gift in the form of a gift certificate for the same amount. He did, and the manager insisted he use the store's bathroom to change and freshen up.

This man who hated books was so impressed that he came back to buy gift certificates at Christmas, Easter, graduation, Mother's Day, Father's Day, and so on. He ended up spending a total of $375 during the following year.

Donald Hess, president of Parisian, often answers his own telephone. He picked it up one day just as he was leaving his office in Birmingham, Alabama, shortly before Christmas. He was scheduled to fly, the next day, out to the Mobile store. The caller said, "Mr. Hess, this is Mark, a sales associate from the Mobile store. You don't know me but I just had a customer come in and she wants a particular sweater for a Christmas gift. She was concerned it might not get here in time if we transferred it. I called the River Chase store [in Birmingham] and I understand they have the item. I understand you are flying down here tomorrow.

"Would you mind going by the store and picking it up, or having someone get it to you so you can bring it to the store tomorrow? It's a white, extra-large Tony Lambert sweater."

Donald couldn't get there himself, but his senior vice president in charge of personnel lived out near the Birmingham store. He was going on the plane with Donald, so he picked it up and brought it with him the next morning. The value of the sale: $36.

The manager of a movie theater in Flagstaff, Arizona, created a triumph strong enough to cause a customer from Tucson to write a letter to the *Arizona Republic*. This man got more than he wanted, and he really loved it just that way.

Editor:

A couple of weeks ago, my wife and I went to see a movie at the Orpheum Theater in Flagstaff. Or was it 30 years ago? Let me explain.

First, as we walked into the lobby, we were greeted by the manager. "Good evening, folks. We've got a good movie; I think you're going to really enjoy it."

Whoa. More than three syllables from a theater employee. Radical.

Next, we bought some popcorn and a soda. Without a co-signer. Pinch me.

Then came the biggie. After the previews were over, the house lights came on and the manager walked down to the front of this giant old full-size-screen movie house. He smiled real big.

"Good evening, folks. Tonight's feature is a very funny family movie, *Look Who's Talking*. I enjoyed it a lot, and I hope you will, too. At the end of the film, you might pay special attention to what happens during the credits. It's really hilarious. Thanks for coming. Enjoy the show."

Everyone applauded . . . a theater employee.

As we left the theater he thanked everyone and asked how they liked the film. My wife and I truly felt as if we were back in the '50s.

I wish that every theater owner, every restaurant owner, every hotel manager, bank president, department store manager—everybody who makes a living serving the paying public—could take in a movie at the Orpheum Theater in Flagstaff.

I'll tell you something. To see somebody who really knows how to appreciate a customer is inspirational, and jarring as hell.

How very much we've lost.

Jay Taylor
Tucson

A FESTIVAL OF FROGS

There are still unspoiled places on the planet, if you care enough to travel far enough, to get there.

It's a long, long way to Fiji, but don't stop at the airport. Near the airport, Fiji is something like San Diego, but it's much too far away to go just for that. You don't want to be spending your best vacation ever in a pool with a swim-up bar with Muzak because your travel agent didn't do a better job.

Instead it is better to wait in the airport for little Sunflower Airlines, which will take you up again, this time over the green mountains and waterfalls of Viti Levu, and on into the sunshine over the outer islands. There are more than three hundred of them. Now every mile enchants your eyes. You land at Savusavu, but stay on the plane. You then fly over the Rainbow Reef in disbelief before you land again at Taveuni. This might be the smallest airport in the world, with a carefully tended garden of about six exquisite flowers. But still you are not "there." You get in a bus which wanders along the coast of Taveuni until it reaches a black sand beach. You now are opposite your destination, and there is a small boat waiting to take you there.

This is a hotel for eighteen guests, but without much in the way of check-in, credit cards, temperature control, frequent-stayer programs, concierge levels, or "Singles Nights." There will be meals and scuba instruction if you want it, and the girls will giggle as they make your bed. If you should want something, there is likely to be someone waiting nearby, but if you don't, there will be nothing visible but the lagoon.

Americans thought up this hotel, but the Fijians built it, and they work there, and they love it. They love their work, and they love their life, and they love you. They line up singing on the beach as your boat approaches, and they will smile, as you cry, when you leave. And you'd better remember to toss your red hibiscus into the water as the boat pulls away, or you will be denying the custom that promises you will return.

The ugly, loud, intrusive modern life is gone.

The service you need now is nature.

Somehow you will learn that if you go for a morning walk between seven and seven-thirty, you'll get to see the snow white blossom show. It lasts only ten minutes, but it happens every day. There is a path lined on both sides with trees that drop their blossoms promptly in the first light of the sun. For about ten minutes the ground is quite covered with fallen white flowers in full bloom. And then they close. Another day has started.

You may even see a couple of Fijians along the path, enjoying watching you enjoy this daily miracle.

Many things are like that out in the corners of Fiji, but what you remember most is the *people* who make you happy there. Service to them is as natural as love, and they give it to you just that way.

They give you things you may not even know you want, such as a wheelbarrow ride from your hut to the main hut for dinner.

Every night the frogs come out. You can hear them, but you cannot see them very well, as they look exactly like the ground they squat on. There are a lot of them. Going anywhere, you could step on them. Or they could step on you as you pass by.

So depending on how you feel about frogs, your otherwise perfect comfort might be tested by your nightly passages between your hut and the big hut dining room.

The woman staying in the hut next to us was terrified of walking through frogs. In fact, these frogs were a matter of consideration to everyone who stayed there, regardless of their usual attitude toward frogs. This customer was faced with a problem. It was either travel through frogs, or starve.

The Fijians spotted this guest with the amphibian crisis. They smiled and huddled until they had the problem solved with such imagination that every night the nerve-wracked customer had the unique round-trip travel experience of her life.

Every day as the sun goes down, the boys play drums around the sacred kava bowl. The flares are lighted, the stars appear, and the fragrant South Seas evening begins. And the frogs come out.

Ten minutes before dinner, Cola and Tomi and George arrived at the hut next door with a wheelbarrow. It had been cleaned and polished and they presented it at my neighbor's steps. And every night in this high island style, this guest was safely wheeled through a minefield of frogs by three hilarious Fijians who created their own fun and happiness by serving a customer.

DO UNTO OTHERS

A young girl at Disneyland spotted trouble in paradise and fixed it instantly. Her customer was standing in a very long line, in a cafeteria that looked a lot like Tahiti. He suddenly dropped a full glass of iced tea on the floor and it smashed, sending pieces flying all over.

This minimum-wage employee immediately set down her broom and dustpan, ran to the head of the line, took another iced tea from behind the counter, ran back to the customer, handed him the tea, retrieved her broom and dustpan, knelt down in front of the customer, and swept up the broken glass, the tea, the ice, and the lemon. She did all this in fifteen seconds. It was a triumph of service!

All the fast food chains have fast food, but McDonald's has fast employees. In Tokyo they all wear buttons that say "Smile!—and hustle!" In Billings, Montana, everything suddenly stops for fifteen seconds while everyone gathers to sing "Happy Birthday" to an *employee*, then they rush back to work. Standardized emotion, to be sure, but what are they singing at Burger King?

There are dozens of everyday triumphs at McDonald's Hamburger University. They beat Kentucky Fried at the chicken game. They listen to their managers for ideas, like inventing the fast-food breakfast. They invent McBarge, the floating restaurant at Expo '86 in Vancouver where all children coming into the restaurant were issued a McDonald's bracelet with a detachable number stub. The parents kept the stub so that any child who got lost and was wearing the bracelet would be instantly matched up with its parents.

But the real reason to buy your french fries at McDonald's instead of anywhere else is because of its service to humanity! The ultimate difference between McDonald's and everybody else is the Ronald McDonald Houses. There are more than one hundred "homes" across the country, usually located near major medical centers, where the families of children who are critically ill can stay with other families during their ordeal—absolutely free.

McDonald's motivates its managers and its employees and its customers, and then goes far beyond to minister to tragedy. At McDonald's, it seems that even life itself *is* their department!

The very best service any of us can ever provide is service to humanity.

Toward the end of my visit to Stew Leonard's, Stew Jr. and I were prowling the floor when he spotted something about a couple in front of us. "I need to see what's going on," he said, and introduced himself to the couple. They were from Colombia, new to the country and the town, had five children, and last night their house had burned to the ground. Everyone now was safe and they were shopping for basics at Stew Leonard's with five hundred dollars that their church had collected for them.

It was "the basics" that did it. Stew Jr. spotted the diapers, milk, bread, salt, peanut butter, paper towels, and toilet paper in their shopping carts, guessed that something unusual was going on, and went over to find out.

Within minutes, three bag boys had appeared. Stew doubled the amount of the groceries the couple chose, at the store's expense, and loaded it all into their car.

Both the idea and the action were done. This couple's misfortune had suddenly become Stew Jr.'s department.

Customers don't ever need to drive more than two miles to get to a drugstore in a city. And all drugstores are almost the same: the same brands, the same unmemorable service, and no one's going to drive one mile farther to save fourteen cents on a bottle of baby oil. So Consumer Value Stores, CVS, drives for its customers. This drugstore chain sends five fully equipped automobile emergency vehicles out on the roads around Boston every day. They are the CVS Good Samaritans and they stop to help disabled cars on the road. Last year they installed life-saving burn foam in the vans in case of car fire where a minute can save a life. The CVS Good Samaritan's mission is to make the "C" sign at customers, outside of their stores, by providing emergency road service. They have received 35,000 letters from customers, thanking them—not just a few of which end with "God Bless You!"

Don't you think those people will drive slightly farther to give back to a CVS drug store what the store once gave to them? Do they talk about it, spreading the word? Does CVS provide customer service?

For fourteen years, the organization called Tree People has been planting trees in California. They have bullied and persuaded governments, corporations, and individuals to join them, even securing the services of prisoners who "do time" by planting trees, and they have planted 1,750,000 trees in California knowing that every tree they plant puts oxygen back into the air.

And Carnie Kline organized an AIDS symposium for Kansas City, enlisting the governor, the mayor, the ad club, $100,000 of free media coverage and publicity, realizing at age thirty-seven what her mother had always meant when she had said, "Carnie, you can do anything you want to!"

Blessed individuals everywhere are acting.

Mother Clara Hale has a brownstone house in Harlem where for the last forty years she has provided love and hope for black infants who are born addicted to drugs.

Anita Roddick, founder of the Body Shop, an international chain of cosmetics stores, was recently nominated International Businesswoman of the Year. Her stores sell products guaranteed never to have been tested on animals. They present educational displays and literature on the ozone layer and other vital environmental causes. Most amazing, it is a requirement that all employees do community service work, for which they are paid. Anita Roddick's Body Shops make an astonishing profit by serving both their customers and the universe.

Ruth Brinker was a retired widow living in San Francisco doing volunteer work cooking and delivering meals to a few friends who had AIDS. One weekend a person who had promised to deliver food to one of Ruth's clients went away for the weekend, forgot to deliver the meals, and the client died.

Ruth was jolted into founding Project Open Hand. She persuaded a local Episcopalian church to assign their kitchen to her, and she put a huge banner up over the stove. The banner read, "Be Not Afraid!" Today Project

Open Hand delivers hundreds of hot, nourishing meals each day to housebound AIDS patients.

And Howard Cooley, president of Jockey International, galvanized the clothing manufacturers of America to send tons of clothing to Armenia within five days after the earthquake.

Justin Lebow, age twelve, believes every kid should have a bike. He spent an average of ten hours each repairing forty bikes and giving them to kids in an orphanage in Saddle Brook, New Jersey. Thanks to stories about his service, Justin has been sent money, parts, and bicycles, and has been offered a job in a local bike shop as soon as he turns fifteen.

In New York City there was a twelve-year-old girl, Cindy, who needed an operation on her spine to correct a potentially crippling congenital defect. There are two different surgical methods to correct this problem. Her father, a tax lawyer, collected the names of twelve different qualified surgeons and then took his daughter to meet and interview the four whose names were most frequently recommended.

He spent a lot of money on office visits, dragging his daughter and her X-rays around with him and discussing with each one of them the technical aspects of the two different procedures and which one was better. It was just as important that his daughter felt comfortable with the doctor who would perform the operation. She rejected one because he didn't look at her during the consultation, talking instead to her father. They picked the one they felt was best and the operation was a success.

Michelle Pugh ran a scuba-equipment rental shop on the beach in St. Croix, but she almost went out of business when pollution drove the fish away and the coral reef lost all its color. Instead of going broke she solicited every restaurant on the island for their extra food, and started luring the fish back to the reefs and, incidentally, tripling her business.

The individual who invented Post-it notes at 3-M, a company which pays its individuals to think, spent eighteen months of mostly his extra time, serving his company and their customers by creating a product that earns the company more than $300 million dollars a year.

Citizens are beginning to fight back on their own, too. Bernhard Goetz, the subway vigilante, shot four muggers in the New York subway, and was indicted for it, but he got a lot of sympathy from the public.

Two men in Detroit, tired of watching a crack house on their street destroy their neighborhood, and frustrated with the lack of response from the local police, set fire to the building and burned it to the ground. They were both prosecuted and publicized. Other "customers" understood and many admired them. The unmotivated like to say, "It's not that bad yet," or, "It could be worse," and they're probably right, it could be worse, and it will be, and maybe then we will all join in the heartfelt cry from the mother of a child murdered in Chicago by crack dealers, who wanted to know, "How long do we have to wait for service?"

People are no more demanding of their government than they are of their local department store. Voter participation gets lower in every election. People have lost their belief in institutions and are turning to themselves. Jeanne Barrett got together with the neighbors on her block in Brooklyn to hire their own police force to counter the dangers of the crack dens in the neighborhood. They pay $240 a day for three shifts. Their "policeman" patrols the block and residents hope that they don't get murdered when these guys need to go to the toilet.

Grandmothers patrol their streets in the Bronx, confronting drug dealers and telling them to "go home." And small unofficial armies of citizen soldiers are forming to fight drugs in the war against crack.

These are all customers making the "C" sign at the state and city services they pay for, but do not get.

The service revolution has begun. Each of these revolutionaries believes, and so should you, that we must live *every* day of our lives.

VII. A NATION
OF FIGHTERS

We were born as a nation of fighters. We staged a revolution and we won. In those days, everything mattered. Everything was worth fighting for. This is the temperament of our beginnings. We were motivated then; we need to be motivated again.

Just imagine what would happen if two hundred and fifty million of us decided to fight instead of whining! What if we all begin to wave the "C" sign and the service revolution succeeds? Service would improve, immediately, and therefore so would business, and our notion of ourselves, and all our pride and action.

One "C" sign at a time, with individual tales of triumph: this is the way a revolution takes place. We don't know if the gas station attendant ever changed his ways after Carole Gilmore gave him the "C" sign, but it does not matter. As Dr. Mattingly said, "I try to get three out of a hundred." And in any case, Carole got her tank filled with gas at the advertised price.

Why bother? Why should we complain and make scenes and waves and rock the boat and constantly fight to get and give good service? Sometimes better airplane food and better theater seats don't seem worth fighting for. But what happens when we accept mediocre police protection, education, and health care? With a mediocre doctor you may die before your time and possibly in greater pain, and that is definitely more important than whether you ever see your luggage again. But the person who fights to find a dedicated teacher is the same person who fights for the table they want in a restaurant. If you don't care where you sit in the Super Bowl, you may not care how you get your chemotherapy, and you may not care, ultimately, about yourself. Caring about better service, about getting and giving it, means caring for yourself.

But if we are to stage a service revolution, we'll need to move quickly from whining and complaining to action. We need to return to our beginnings and once again become a nation of fighters.

We *must* do the *best* we can.

Bad service isn't all we've got to deal with. We've got a bad economy, poverty, illiteracy, homelessness, nuclear activity and toxic waste, air pollution, overpopulation, drugs and crime and violence, and too much trash.

And we whine, or we complain, and we wish it wasn't happening. It's not exactly my problem, it's not my table, it's not my job, or myself, or my life, or my planet: "*It's not my department!*"

And all the while we know that, once again, if we don't fight, we'll never win.

> *This is the way the world ends*
> *Not with a bang but a whimper.*

The overwhelming issue facing humanity today and from now on is the fate of our planet. Every other issue depends on it. Some say the Earth has ten years to go, some more, some less. Wouldn't it be "service" to save it?

The earth needs "service"—a service yet to come which will affect us all, and which could save us. We live here as a privilege, in good health, served by a planet with a perfect immune system—our environment. Our planet has always served us, unconditionally, asking nothing back.

But we have seldom served the Earth. Instead we have infected it, and now we inhabit a planet in critical condition, fighting for its life.

The Earth is suffering a plague of fevers, a body much too hot and much too cold. The Earth is much too dry: Crops fail, and species and people die. The Earth is much too wet: The ice caps melt and now the newly swollen oceans rise up high to meet the toxic air of acid rain. Now floods, volcanoes, hurricanes, and earthquakes shake the planet. The skin of the Earth is exposed to radiation through a large and growing ozone hole, a lesion in the heavens. The unprotected surface bakes, so plants don't grow. We burn our forest lungs and so the Earth has difficulty breathing. The regular rhythm is broken and all predictions falter. We stand by while the sun goes down and we admire the sunset caused by chemicals. Our environmental immune system has begun to fail. We are living with a planet that is spoiling day by day, dying a little at a time.

We must save the Earth, or it will die. It is now our turn to serve the Earth. We must become providers. We are finally about to be motivated—in the surest way we are ever moved to action—by *absolute necessity*. We must become fighters again. Good planets are hard to find.

It's a very long distance from a single customer making a "C" sign in a gas station to the prospect of six billion people united in saving the Earth. But we get there exactly the same way: fighting.

This is the biggest fight that lies ahead for all of us. In this fight, there will be no "sides," no enemies (except indifference), and no excuses.

We must create a unified world of fighters. This will require every individual, and each inhabitant of every neighborhood, and every nation in the world, in universal cooperation, peacefully, one by one and everyone, one "C" sign at a time, until six billion of us fight together, to save the planet and ourselves.

The Earth is everyone's department.

This is the "service" that matters most.

This is the only service that can give us back our future, and lead us to a time of possibilities and joy.

APPENDIX

The following is a list of Peter Glen's clients and activities from 1980 through 1990.

Peter Glen thanks them all for their continuing inspiration.

RETAILERS

Army and Air Force Exchange
  Service
Belk's
Bloomingdale's
Britches of Georgetown
Camelot Enterprises
Canadian Tire Corp.
Chess King
Color Tile Inc.
Conran's Habitat
Consumer Value Stores
Dayton-Hudson Corp.
Duty Free Shoppers
Dylex
Eaton's
Eckerd Drugs
Eddie Bauer
Erol's Video
Hartmarx
Heilig-Myers
Hess'
Host Marriott
Hudson's Bay Co.
Le Chateau

Lipton's
Littman's Jewelers
Matsuya Japan
Meldisco
Melville Corporation
Mervyn's
Miller's Outpost
Nationwide Television
P. A. Bergner & Co.
Parisian
RKO Warner Video
Scandia Down Corp.
Sears
Steiger's
Sterling Inc.
Target Stores
The Bombay Company
The Gap
The May Company
This End Up
Thom McAn
Waldenbooks

Wherehouse Entertainment
Wohl Shoe Co.

ASSOCIATIONS/ CONFERENCES

Action Sports Retailers
American Footwear Industries Association
American Formalwear Association
American Institute of Floral Designers
Bank Marketing Association
British Video Association
Canadian National Development Agency
Dallas Market Center Co.
Exhibit Designers and Producers Association
Financial Institutions Marketing Association
Illinois Retail Merchants Association
Independent Retailers Syndicate
Institute of Business Design
Institute of Store Planners
Interbike Expo
Intercontinental Department Stores Association
International Council of Shopping Centers
International Newspaper Marketing Association
Japan Department Stores Association
Manstyle Canada
Marketing Focus Australia
Men's Fashion Association

Menswear Retailers of America
Morgan Stanley Retail Forum
National Association of Chain Drug Stores
National Association of Display Industries
National Association of Music Merchants
National Association of Record Merchants
National Home Furnishings Association
National Mass Retailers Association
New Zealand Retail Federation
Professional Association of Diving Instructors
Radio Bureau of Canada
Retail Advertising and Marketing Association
Retail Advertising Conference
Retail Council of British Columbia
Sherry Cassin and Co.
Ski Industries of America
Store Planning Equipment Services Seminar
The Fashion Group
Western Association of Visual Merchandising

REAL ESTATE AND SHOPPING CENTER DEVELOPERS

Cadillac Fairview
Corporate Property Investors
Crown American
Enterprise Development
JMB Realty

May Centers
Melvin Simon and Associates Inc.
New England Development
Pembrook Management Inc.
Robert B. Aikens Associates Inc.
The Hahn Co.
The Rouse Company
The Taubman Co.
Westcor Partners

MEDIA COMPANIES

Arizona Republic and *Phoenix Gazette*
Details magazine
K103 FM Portland
Radio Bureau of Canada
The Chicago Tribune
Union Tribune Publishing Co.

MANUFACTURERS

Albert Nipon
Bulova Watch Co.
Caltex New Zealand
CBS-Fox Video
Dan River Mills
Esprit
General Foods
Mitsubishi Electric
Munsingwear
Nike
Phillips-Van Heusen
Red Cross Shoes
Sanyo Electric Inc.
Sun Ice

Swank
The Coppley Group
The North Face
Thomasville Furniture
Timex
Union Underwear
West Point Pepperell

AGENCIES/SUPPLIERS

ADVO-Systems Inc.
General Electric Capital
John Ryan and Co.
Saffer Advertising Inc.
STS Systems
The Results Group

TEACHING

Georgetown University

PROJECTS

"90 Minutes for Life"—AIDS
benefit

RETAIL STORE

Flatiron, New York

WRITING

It's Not My Department!

Visual Merchandising / Store Design magazine

INDEX

ABOUT
THE AUTHOR

Peter Glen is an outspoken advocate of customer rights and service. Peter saw the need for a revolution in service while he was attending high school in Michigan and working as a clerk in a small-town jewelry store. One summer a theater group came to town and when they left, Peter went with them. At the University of Arizona, he became an actor.

He soon realized that "retailing is theater." He returned to Michigan to run the family factory store, where he developed unusual techniques for selling, presentation, and service. And he sold sportswear on the road in Georgia and Alabama.

Discovering that fulfillment did not lie in selling sportswear in the South, Peter went to Australia. There, for the next two years, he traveled thousands of miles throughout the South Pacific presenting unique fashion shows and motivating salespeople in stores.

Being successful in Australia doesn't guarantee you anything in New York. Peter discovered this when he returned home and established his own business, Peter Glen Inc. No one would hire him. Peter had forty-five interviews with moguls in the fashion industry. No one would hire him.

Just before starving or, worse yet, having to consider getting a regular job, Peter was hired by a risk-taking children's-wear manufacturer to entertain and motivate department store salespeople at one of its premier accounts, Rich's in Atlanta, Georgia.

Fueled by excitement and despair, the presentation was such a success that the store itself immediately hired Peter to present seminars to all of its stores. The next year, Peter performed in twenty leading department stores. It soon became clear that what worked to motivate retailers also worked for manufacturers, airlines, hotels, banks, hospitals, schools, and any other business in which money is exchanged by customers for service.

During the last twenty-five years, Peter has traveled, explored, photographed, prepared, and presented ideas and inspiration. He has given over twenty-five hundred performances to more than a million people. Peter reaches still others through videotapes and writing, and is recognized as America's foremost customer.

Peter's presentations change with events, which should teach providers to react to changing customer interests and demands. His ambition is constant, however: to motivate the fight to do the best one can for the improvement of both business and life. Peter endeavors to inspire the business of business and is currently concerned with the quality of service to the earth.

As the standards of service and the quality of life decline, the necessity of bringing customers and providers of services closer together for their common good is more urgent than ever before.

The way to raising the standards of customer service requires nothing less than a revolution in attitudes and commitment. Peter Glen believes that when this revolution is finally accomplished, the way to a better existence will have been discovered to be through service to the world, through caring and involvement and action, and by *living* every day of our lives.